The San Juan Islands

AFOOT & AFLOAT

Text and maps by Marge Mueller
Photos by Marge and Ted Mueller

The Mountaineers • Seattle

THE MOUNTAINEERS
Organized 1906

To explore and study the mountains, forests and watercourses of the
Northwest;

To gather into permanent form the history and traditions of this
region;

To preserve by the encouragement of protective legislation or
otherwise the natural beauty of Northwest America;

To make explorations into these regions in fulfillment of the above
purposes;

To encourage a spirit of good fellowship among all lovers of outdoor
life.

Copyright © 1979 by Marge Mueller. All rights reserved.
Published by
The Mountaineers, 719 Pike Street, Seattle, Washington 98101
Distributed in Canada by
Douglas & McIntyre Ltd., 1875 Welch Street, North Vancouver, B.C. V7P 1B7
Manufactured in the United States of America

Edited by Peggy Ferber, book design by Marge Mueller

PHOTO CREDITS
Bob and Ira Spring: Pages 26, 60, 63, 70, 79, 88, 89, 91, 96, 112, 139, 146, 177, 191,
194, 211, 214
Ken Balcomb—Orca Survey: Page 107

Cover photos: (top) Sunrise on Padilla Bay, Fidalgo Island—Mt. Baker on left; (middle)
Fox Cove, Sucia Island; (bottom) Cascade Lake Trail, Moran State Park, Orcas Island
Title Photo: Ferry in Harney Channel. Obstruction and Peavine Passes in the distance,
Mt. Baker on the skyline

Mueller, Marge
    The San Juan Islands, afoot and afloat.

    Includes index.
    1. San Juan Islands—Description and travel—Guide-
books. I. Title.
F897.S2M79 1979   917.97'74   78-54424
ISBN 0-916890-63-5

FOREWORD

SAN JUAN RECREATION—AFOOT OR AFLOAT? OR MAYBE BOTH!

Reader, please note: this is a *recreation guide*, not an *island guide*. Although this fact may not always be apparent from reading through these pages, it must be established that the major emphasis of this book lies in the things to do in the San Juans, and the enjoyment which can be had in doing them.

At the same time it is recognized that any visitor to the San Juans needs to have at least a general idea of what to expect in the way of amenities. Commercial facilities listed in this book are mentioned primarily on a "need-to-know" basis, such as where to find food, lodging, fuel, moorage and other necessities.

If a visitor is interested in specifics regarding island facilities, a number of tourist and commercial publications are available which list names, addresses and phone numbers of businesses in the islands. The **San Juan Islands Almanac,** which is published annually, includes a comprehensive business directory.

As its title indicates, this book deals with the broad spectrum of good, clean, healthy, active and largely non-polluting recreation available in the San Juan Islands, either on land or on water. Yet the reader thumbing through these pages for his favorite sport will soon note that island recreation does not divide itself into such two neat categories, for some hikes and campgrounds are accessible only by boat, fishing can be from either boat or land, scuba diving can be boat or shore-based, and many beaches can be reached either by land or sea. And to achieve a catchy title, bicycling was not implied at all, although it certainly is one of the most delightful pastimes in the San Juans, and one that is frequently mentioned here.

The recreations discussed are active, "doing" sorts of things, but they are also take-it-easy, stop-and-smell-the-flowers divertissements. The islands aren't very big; one could rush through the larger ones in a day and claim to have "seen" the San Juans. In this book the reader is urged to stop and think about the history of the Indians who first arrived here in long cedar canoes, and the Spaniards and Englishmen who came later in sailing ships. Take time to notice the unique birds and flowers and animals and the special quality of the clouds piled high above the long, horizontal reaches of the islands. The more you look, the more there is to see.

BOATING

Boating in the San Juans is such a broad category, indulged in by so many people in so many different ways that it becomes difficult to discuss. Cruisers have one point of view, sailors another, fishermen another and kayakers yet another. Perhaps it should be stated here that this author is a sailor, and thus especially concerned about such unpleasant things as scraping keels across rocks and running aground (and perhaps also accounting for the take-it-easy point of view).

Comments regarding boating are as general as possible, touching on as many situations as possible; however, in no way can this book supplant a *good, nautical chart* and boating know-how. Charts covering San Juan waters are listed in the back of this book.

There are many hazards, both in the islands and inherent to boating. Before attempting any cruising, boaters are urged to take a boating safety course. The U.S. Power Squadron's classes in small boat handling are excellent; information regarding the course can be obtained through the U.S. Coast Guard.

In many places throughout the text cautionary comments refer to "small boats", a vague category including dinghys, rubber rafts, canoes and kayaks, or in general, any water craft that is paddled or has minimal power. These cautions can also apply to boaters in larger boats who have had little experience in handling adverse conditions, whatever the size of craft, for they too should use extra care in navigating San Juan waters.

Many canoe and kayak trips are possible in the San Juans, ranging from quiet paddles around protected bays to extended open water excursions. Canoeists and kayakers should have training in ocean traveling before attempting any open water trips, and *any* boater, before beginning any trip, should check on local weather conditions.

Tidal currents in the San Juans vary from one to ten knots; the more severe currents can cause small boaters serious problems, and a strong beam tide can even create difficulties for larger boats navigating in a dense fog.

Tidal current *is not the same as the tide,* although one does give rise to the other. Tides measure the vertical distance water rises and falls above the sea floor, while tidal currents represent the horizontal flow of water resulting from the rise and fall of the tide.

Tidal current tables (*not* tide tables), which are printed annually, are keyed to station points on the small craft portfolio charts. The approximate time of maximum velocity of the current can be computed by referencing the tidal current tables to the station point. Although many other factors do enter into the actual surface velocity, and even the direction of the current, general knowledge of the predicted current is invaluable to safe navigation.

FISHING

The state of Washington requires licenses for both saltwater salmon fishing and freshwater fishing. Licenses are not needed for other types of saltwater angling. The water around the San Juan Islands is open to fishing year around; be sure to check state regulations for possession limits and other restrictions.

Some of the lakes in San Juan and Skagit Counties are open year around, others have seasons. A brochure published by the State Department of Game lists all regulations and seasons. Lakes within the state parks are subject to these same restrictions.

SCUBA DIVING AND BEACHCOMBING

Scuba divers, beach users, and boaters trapping crab and shrimp must observe all state regulations on the taking of fish, shellfish and any other food animal. The saltwater sport fishing pamphlet, published by the State Department of Fisheries, which is available in most sporting goods stores, lists bag limits and other restrictions.

After digging clams, fill all holes. It may take several turns of the tide for displaced sand to be leveled. In the meantime small marine animals trapped in the pile may smother, or others exposed to the sun may die of exposure.

Capturing crabs at Shallow Bay, Sucia Island

All of the seashores and seabed of San Juan County and around Cypress Island in Skagit County are a marine biological preserve. The taking or destruction of any living specimen, except for food use, is prohibited by state law. Special permission may be granted in the case of scientific research; such permission may be obtained by writing the Director of the Friday Harbor Laboratories, P.O. Box 459, Friday Harbor, Washington, 98250.

Empty seashells, small rocks and driftwood may be taken by beachcombers, although many of them harbor tiny marine life. Check to see if it's inhabited before taking it home. Overzealous beachcombers are often seen hauling off buckets of beach treasures. Most of it is eventually discarded in someone's back yard. While there is certainly pleasure in having a small souvenir of a San Juan trip on a coffee table or mantel, please use restraint in the quantity you take.

Several publications are available which give suggestions on digging clams and catching crabs and shrimp. Two small, paperback books, **How to Catch Shellfish**, by Charles White and Nelson Dewey, and **How to Catch Crabs**, by Cap'n Crabwelle, are excellent.

WALKING, HIKING AND BICYCLING

Roads in the San Juans are narrow, often without shoulders. Although traffic usually is light, care must be used to not endanger yourself and drivers. Walk on the left, facing on-coming traffic, but bike single-file on the right, moving with traffic. Stop to rest only where there are turnouts, *not* on the narrow shoulder, on hills, curves or in ditches. Wear light colored and bright clothing so that you are easily seen. Flags are an excellent addition to bicycles.

Restrooms are often few and far between in the rural areas—plan ahead. "Taking to the woods" is often trespassing.

CAMPING

In addition to city, county and state parks which have camping areas, a number of resorts also have campgrounds. Check for space as soon as you arrive at your destination, and go elsewhere if accommodations are not available. Campground managers will usually be helpful in suggesting alternatives, and sometimes will call around to help you find a place for the night.

ACKNOWLEDGMENTS

Thanks are unquestionably due to the many people whose encouragement and assistance helped in the creation of this book. Credit must first go to my husband, Ted, who offered suggestions, criticism and unending moral support—this is as much his book as it is mine. Thanks also to my children, Craig and Heidi, who were photographer's models and research assistants *par excellence,* and who followed me faithfully along many an overgrown trail, despite their conviction that Mom was hopelessly lost.

After my family, the debt to Ira Spring is enormous, for he gave invaluable help in the selection of the photos, and lent his darkroom expertise in the printing of many of them.

Gratitude is also due the many people in organizations and government agencies who supplied information and checked sections of the manuscript for accuracy: Drs. Dennis Willows and Richard Strathmann of the Friday Harbor Laboratories; State Park Rangers Wil Lorentz, Doug Pesznecker, Bill Byrne, Dave Hoffman, Dave Shannon, Ralph Mast and Sally Straathof; William A. Bush of the State Parks and Recreation Commission; Superintendent S. J. Zachwieja of San Juan National Historical Park; A. R. O'Donnell and Harold Villager of the Department of Natural Resources; Willard Hesselbart of the U.S. Fish and Wildlife Service; and Prentiss Bloedel and Bob Pyle of the Nature Conservancy.

And finally, thanks to Peggy Ferber, John Pollock and Donna DeShazo of The Mountaineers • Books—to Peggy for her work as my editor, and to John and Donna for their enthusiasm and encouragement at the beginning of this project and for their cajolery, brow-beating and psychological ploys to help me finally bring this manuscript to completion.

MARGE MUELLER

INTRODUCTION

Tucked away in the far northwest corner of the state of Washington, a cluster of emerald gems, set in shimmering azure, lie like a sequestered treasure, awaiting a very special, quiet time to be taken out, examined and enjoyed.

Tops of an ancient mountain range, which over eons settled and became inundated by the sea, the islands were sculpted by massive glacial ice sheets which completely covered them, grinding off tall peaks, gouging out watery channels and estuaries, and depositing great, smooth piles of gravelly debris.

Only the granite hearts of the mountains remain, still bearing the marks of the glacier's southward journey. Soft glacial till in lowlands has fostered the growth of forests, flowered meadows and thickets. Wind and water buffeting mile upon mile of coastline carved myriad shapes, from wide, marine life-teeming, bay bottom tide flats and long, curving, golden sand spits to narrow, wave-cut bedrock benches.

By definition the San Juans are generally accepted as being those islands lying north of the Straits of Juan de Fuca, south and east of the Canadian boundary and west of—aye, there's the rub! Where do we draw the eastern boundary? San Juan County uses Rosario Strait as its line of demarcation, but islands eastward ache to be called San Juans, too, and with some reason.

By geological and historical heritage, if not by bureaucratic boundaries, Cypress, Guemes and Fidalgo are certainly of the same family. And so, for that reason, and for purposes of convenience, all of the islands of Skagit County will be considered as San Juan Islands here.

Indeed the Skagit County islands serve as an entrance, since a majority of the traffic passes among them, either on the ferry from Anacortes, or through Deception Pass or the Swinomish Channel. And it is here that a visitor first sees the forested hills reaching down to placid bays, and rock buttresses enclosing narrow, silvery channels which characterize this ultimate melding of land and water.

And how many islands are there? As difficult as the territory may be to define, it's even harder to catalog. Figures range from 172 to more than 700! If that seems a startling discrepancy, consider when is an island merely a rock? How many rocks make a reef? Is a reef an island? What about tidal changes which cause rocks and reefs to appear or disappear and split apart or join together? The problems are legion.

The figure of 172 theoretically includes all those named islands or groups of islands within San Juan County, but don't try to count them — you'll never come out with that number. But as stated, this book also includes the islands of Skagit County as San Juans, so for now let's say "around 200", and go on to other things.

GETTING AROUND IS HALF THE FUN

A watery highway system of broad straits and fjord-like channels links these many islands. Green and white ferries cruise the waters, busily "bussing" people and vehicles and bicycles and trailered or car-topped boats from island to island. All ferry routes begin at the city of Anacortes on Fidalgo Island and usually stop at four of the larger islands, Lopez, Shaw, Orcas and San Juan, occasionally continuing on across Haro Strait to Sidney, B.C. on Vancouver Island.

Shaw Island from the Washington State ferry

Passengers enjoy what is advertised as "the most scenic ferry ride in the world", from picture windows in the comfort of the ferry's interior, or from breezy open decks, like balconies above the water. At times the vista is a broad panorama of sparkling sea and receding layers of gray-green islands backed by snow-capped distant mountains. Other times rugged rock-bound shores seem within touching distance as the ferry threads through narrow passes. Depending on the season and the luck and sharp eye of the observer, jumping salmon, seals, soaring eagles, great flocks of migrating ducks or even a pod of killer whales may be seen. At each time of day, each change of weather, each advance of season, the islands are painted in infinite variety—the vivid hues of a perfect summer day, the drifting mists of a spring-time fog, the brilliant fire of an evening sunset.

Of course private boats, too, travel these waterways—do they ever! Seeking nirvana in salt-scrubbed air and crystal water and tranquil anchorages, they arrive, drove upon drove. Unfettered by such things as stodgy ferry schedules, they wander freely among the islands, visiting big and little, particularly the numerous boat-in marine state parks.

But these non-ferry-served islands are not reserved for affluent yacht owners alone. Even a canoe or rowboat will do to reach some, for several of the state parks lie in protected bays within paddling distance. Islands across broader channels can be reached by boats brought via the ferry to launch spots on the larger islands; marinas within the San Juans offer a wide variety of boats to be rented for the hour or day, or chartered for week-long cruises.

Most of the larger islands have single-landing-strip airfields, and San Juan Airlines maintains a regular schedule year-around to these airports, with added flights in the summer. Stops are made by prior reservation only. Several air services, based at San Juan, Lopez and Fidalgo Islands, charter either small land or seaplanes for flights throughout the islands. Seaplane floats are maintained at Friday Harbor and Roche Harbor.

Many tourists leave their automobiles in the parking lot at Anacortes and walk on the ferry with bicycle or backpack and hiking boots, prepared to enjoy the islands to the fullest at a slower pace. Roads on the ferry-served islands are gently rolling, traffic is light, and the slow and quiet traveler will see far more wildlife and far more beauty than those who rush from here to there in automobiles. Some campgrounds have special areas set aside for hikers and bikers.

THE FLY IN THE OINTMENT

Most paradises have their flaws, and unfortunately the San Juans have theirs, for they are loved almost too much and they can be crowded—exasperatingly crowded! Long ferry lines can mean up to a three-hour wait for car passengers, overnight accommodations can be filled, marinas can be badly congested and parks can be overflowing with people—from June to September.

After Labor Day the tourist crowds almost magically disappear and, except for an occasional sunny winter holiday, the islands are returned to their grateful residents. So be forewarned—expect to wait in a ferry line, have reservations for overnight accommodations and realize that campgrounds may be filled and you will have to go elsewhere (signs attempt to notify prospective campers of this before they board the ferry in Anacortes).

Is it worth it? You bet it is! But you must be prepared to be patient and relax (that's one of the great secrets of the island magic). If the ferry leaves you at the dock, there's always another one soon, and no matter how many people there are, the scenery is big enough for everyone to share.

Does that mean the islands aren't any good off-season? Shhh—that's the best kept secret of all. They're often better. The mobs are gone (but won't be if the secret ever gets out), and although the weather's cooler and a bit more unpredictable, on a crisp fall day when Indian summer paints the forests, or a blustery winter day when awesome waves lash at beaches, or a damp spring day when wildflowers fill hedgerows and new-born lambs cavort in fields, the islands truly show the many subtle nuances of their beauty.

SO YOU'VE DECIDED ON THE FERRY RIDE — HERE'S HOW TO DO IT

For the novice ferry user, the system may at times seem bewildering; even for the experienced ferry commuter accustomed to cross-sound runs, the procedure in the San Juans is a bit different.

Three types of runs operate through the islands—the domestic, the interisland and the international. In summer departures are about hourly; all stops are scheduled. Confusing? It certainly can be. Just remember that not all ferries make all stops, and it is up to you to be sure you are on the right one. Read the ferry schedule carefully, and when in doubt ask the ticket agent.

Ferry schedules which, by the way, change quarterly, are available at the various ferry terminals and oftentimes at businesses in any of the Washington State Ferry-served cities. Schedules and other information can also be obtained by writing to: Washington State Ferries, Pier 52, Seattle, Washington 98104, or by telephoning the number listed in the back of this book.

WALK-ON PASSENGERS. Riding the ferry is a simple matter if traveling by foot—simply buy a ticket and walk on board when the boat arrives, relax by a window and enjoy the beautiful ride—no wait, no hassle, and very inexpensive. If you purchase a round trip ticket you may spend the day cruising through the islands, enjoying the changing scene from the comfort of the ferry, not even bothering to go ashore.

BICYCLES. This increasingly popular mode of transportation causes little problem on the ferries, either, although there are some who wonder if the day won't come that a ferry will be so filled with bicycles that there won't be any room for cars at all. There is only a small additional charge for bicycles. Passengers are responsible for loading, unloading and for the safety of their own equipment.

Bicycles are usually loaded and unloaded as a group, ahead of the four-wheeled vehicles; follow the directions of the ferry crew. After leaving the boat, be aware that a long line of vehicles with some possibly frazzled drivers are coming right behind you. Stay well to the side so you don't hold them up.

VEHICLES. Oh, you want to take you *car*, well, that's another matter. The first question is—won't you reconsider? Will you really need it on the island? Call ahead to see what transportation arrangements can be worked out, for there are many alternatives. If visiting friends, perhaps they will pick you up at the terminal; some resorts will meet their customers and drive them to their destination; if you are chartering a boat the same arrangements may be possible. Or consider car-pooling with a friend. Taxi service is available on Orcas Island.

However, if you're convinced your car or camper is necessary, remember that ferry travel by car can be a delight or an aggravation—it depends largely on the frame of mind of the traveler. If you anticipate waiting in line, take along a book to read (this one is highly recommended), a pillow to take a nap, or a deck of cards to play games with the kids. Several of the ferry landings have restaurants overlooking the terminal where passengers can get a sandwich and a cup of coffee while waiting. Get out and walk around, browse through nearby shops, but don't stray too far, for at times during peak traffic hours an extra ferry will be put into service, and it may appear without warning. Ferry schedules are often loose during time of heavy traffic, as the boats hurry to provide maximum service. Be alert for ferry arrivals and departures.

A reservation system would be the ideal solution, unfortunately no workable system has yet been devised that would be fair to both residents and visitors, taking into account the complexity of loading for multiple destinations.

To achieve smooth and quick unloading, cars are assigned lanes at the landing, at the time of purchasing tickets. Do not be upset if later-arriving cars are assigned to shorter lanes. Space on the ferries is apportioned, depending on typical traffic, with more spaces allowed for Orcas and San Juan Islands, and fewer for Lopez and Shaw. The system is as fair as possible.

At times the ferry will leave the dock with cars still waiting, but open space obvious. This is done only when it is necessary to save room for cars already waiting on another island.

The ferry agent will ask you your destination; follow his directions exactly. If you plan to stop at one island before continuing on to another, be sure that you are parked in the lane for your *first* destination, not your final one.

Other than at Anacortes, car passengers must park first and walk to the ferry landing to purchase tickets. The lanes are usually signed by destination, however always check with the agent to see that you are correctly parked. If you arrive quite early the ticket office may not be open; when it is opened, be sure to find out if you are parked correctly.

Most important of all—don't try to crash the line. In addition to being in very bad taste, it can be injurious to your health. After waiting in line for more than an hour, passengers have been known to become pretty irate at people who do not play by the rules, and fist fights have occurred. While this type of retaliation is certainly not recommended, be forewarned—it can happen.

The word is, relax, be patient and courteous, stay alert and follow directions. Ferry employees have a monumental task in properly loading cars for the various destinations and assuring that space is fairly allocated to all. Don't hassle them, they know what they're doing. Aside from medical emergencies they cannot grant special favors to passengers.

Peak hours are in the early morning and early evening. Busiest days are Friday through Sunday and, of course, holidays. If possible avoid these times.

OVERSIZED VEHICLES. There is an extra charge for large RVs, vacation trailers and trailered boats. In addition, there is only limited space alloted for parking large vehicles, so it is possible that during peak hours there may be a longer wait if you drive this type of camper. Ferry attendants try to load as many customers as possible. It is easier for them to shoehorn in six Volkswagens and Toyotas than one pick-up camper pulling a boat.

Now that you've made it on board you may leave your car and go topside to enjoy the most scenic boat ride in the world. The loudspeaker will announce when your destination is near, giving you ample time to return to your car.

OF "NO TRESPASSING" SIGNS AND OTHER AGGRAVATIONS

One of the most negative aspects of the San Juans, and most noticeable to those of us devoted to good, clean public recreation, and lots of it, is the proliferation of "No Trespassing" signs throughout San Juan County. They seem to spring from every fence post and every beach, screaming, "Stay away, we don't want you here!" Under such duress the meek become paranoid and the feisty grow defiant.

San Juan residents aren't unfriendly—in fact they're some of the nicest folks around, and most of them feel that tourism is a vital function of their islands. These people are simply tired of boorish boaters who come ashore to relieve themselves and their dogs on private beaches, leaving feces and toilet paper strewn about; they're tired of fences ripped down and campfires built in dry timber and grasslands by campers; they're tired of farm animals shot and children endangered by overzealous hunters; they're tired of ignorant disregard of privacy and outright vandalism and thievery.

The horror stories are plentiful—enough to make fellow-tourists ashamed of their breed. But we know we're not all like that, in fact darned few of us are, so don't take "No Trespassing" signs as a personal afront. Instead, respect them and the rights of the people who own property, who keep the islands functioning with their tax money, and who are doing their best to keep it unspoiled for the future.

Even if lands are unposted, do not assume that they are public, or that no one cares if you trespass. Unless clearly designated as public land, *stay off*, somebody owns it. The growth of public recreation in the San Juans lies largely in the hands of the residents. More lands are available for development now, and more could become available in the future, but it will take a favorable position by these residents, convinced that tourism is really good for their economy and not a financial drain requiring more roads and more police and fire protection (paid for out of *their* taxes), before there is any marked increase in public recreation facilities.

With a growth rate far greater than any other Washington county, increasing nearly 74% in the last eight years, San Juan County has trouble coping with the pressures created by its own residents, let alone hordes of visitors. Many ask, how far can the islands stretch? Is there a limit to how many can be accommodated? With an educated, cooperative attitude tourists can minimize their impact on these islands, and somewhat ease the pressures.

WATER. "Water, water, everywhere, but not a drop to drink," may soon become the theme of the San Juans, for at present there's barely enough to go around. Some of the small marine park islands have none at all, and wells at several of the other parks frequently run dry by mid-summer. Even in the towns water is at a premium, with new construction of homes and businesses limited in some areas by the unavailability of water hook-ups. Heavy demands on wells and catch basins are causing these water resources to be depleted.

As ridiculous as it may sound, when visiting the San Juans, *bring water*! Fill up camper and boat water tanks at home or at the last mainland stop, and once you're there, take it easy. There's enough water at present to assure reasonable cleanliness for everyone, but don't let faucets run unnecessarily at campgrounds, don't rinse down boats with fresh water at marinas, and don't use a gallon of water when a quart will do.

FIRE. Going hand-in-hand with the water problem in the islands is the problem of serious fires. There are no convenient fire hydrants on every street corner (and very few street corners). In remote areas reaching a fire is very difficult, and putting it out more so. By late summer, roadside grasses and thickets can be tinder dry, so please be extremely careful with matches, cigarettes and campfires.

GARBAGE. Trash disposal is a growing problem here—literally. Land is so precious that little can be devoted to "sanitary landfill", and shipping it off-island is an expensive proposition. Attempts are being made at running recycling stations on San Juan and Orcas Islands. Thoughtful visitors could consider sorting their trash and dropping off recyclables at these centers. If at all possible, take the rest back home with you.

PETS. It may come as a rude surprise, but dear Fido is not exactly welcome in the San Juans. In this largely rural country, city dogs and farm animals often do not mix well, and every year there are many tragic instances of domestic animals being slaughtered by dogs roaming free. The perpetrators were not vicious watch dogs, trained to attack, but friendly, sit-by-the-fire family pets.

The San Juan County dog ordinance states that any unlicensed dog found at large in rural areas may be shot. This applies to dogs of residents and visitors alike. Leave your pet at home or keep him on a leash.

PUBLIC LANDS

Public-owned lands in the San Juans are a calico-quilt of city, county, state and national parks, lands owned by the state Department of Natural Resources (DNR), Coast Guard-maintained lighthouses owned by the U.S. Bureau of Land Management, fishing lakes owned by the State Department of Game, and wildlife refuges operated by the U.S. Fish and Wildlife Service. In addition, The Nature Conservancy, which is a private conservation organization, supported by

Sunrise on Padilla Bay; Mt. Baker in distance

public memberships and donations, has purchased some property in the islands.

This public property presently totals in excess of 12,000 acres, scattered about more than fifty separate locations (wildlife refuges are an additional eighty four sites). All of these lands except the wildlife refuges (which have three exceptions which will be noted later) and the lighthouse reserves are open to public recreation. Facilities vary from excellent parks with complete camping facilities to primitive patches of land with no improvements whatsoever.

The public sites together offer a rich variety of recreation—boating, fishing, scuba diving, beachcombing, shellfish gathering, hiking, bird watching, camping, sightseeing and many other activities.

Rules and regulations in the various areas are set up to preserve the natural environment and to maintain the safety and pleasure of all visitors. The observance of these regulations is especially important in San Juan County, where many local residents view public-use lands with an uneasy eye, fearing that public abuse of such lands will flow over to neighboring private property. Additionally, many long-time islanders have a strong paternal feeling toward these areas, for they loved and cared for them long before any mainland tourist ever set foot on them.

THE PARKS—CITY, COUNTY AND STATE
(RULES, REGULATIONS AND COURTESY)

The following comments apply specifically to the parks in the San Juans operated by the Washington State Parks and Recreation Commission. In general, these same rules, where relevant, also apply to city, county and DNR parks. Many of the parks have specific rules and regulations prominently posted on a bulletin board, or have pamphlets available at park headquarters. Check local regulations when using any area.

All San Juan DNR recreation areas are maintained by State Parks personnel, by joint agreement of the two agencies. This arrangement provides more efficient servicing of the camp areas.

Some activities listed here may not be specifically covered by park regulations, but many do affect the aesthetics of the area and the enjoyment of others. While visiting, be courteous and considerate of other park users and treat the park itself with care. It is not the wish to set down a long, pedantic list of "don'ts" here, in order to restrict the freedom and pleasure of recreationists, but it must be recognized that in any public-use facility one must bend a little to the needs of others, perhaps sacrificing some individual freedom for the benefit of all.

CAMPING. Camp only in designated areas; camping is limited to seven consecutive days. Do not ditch tents, cut green boughs for beds, hammer nails into trees or in any other way mutilate nature in the quest for a perfect campsite.

GARBAGE. Trash cans are provided in all but the undeveloped state parks. Please use them, rather than depositing litter on the beaches or in campgrounds; however, with the increasing waste disposal problem in the San Juans, a sensitive visitor will take his garbage back home with him whenever possible. In areas where garbage cans are not provided. all trash *must* be removed.

When on boats, do not "deep six" debris, whether it is beverage containers, orange peels or chicken bones. It does not usually come to rest six fathoms down, but will eventually wash up on some beach as ugly litter.

FIRES. Build fires only in designated fireplaces and fire rings. This park regulation is vitally important due to the extreme fire hazard during the summer months, and the difficulty of handling fires on the remote islands. Before leaving, be sure your camp fire is out. Beach fires are prohibited in order to maintain the beaches in a nearly natural state. Report any out-of-control fire immediately—see the Emergency section in the back of this book.

Some boaters cook on portable charcoal-burning barbeques or hibachis, which they place on the float, alongside their boat. Such cookers have badly charred some of the docks; when using any such stove on the dock be sure that the wood is properly shielded from the heat of the cooker.

DRIFTWOOD. Small pieces of driftwood may be taken from the beaches for use in fireplaces, however the use of a chainsaw for the cutting of wood is discouraged, and in some parks is prohibited. State law forbids the removal from beaches any logs which are considered "marketable", except by licensed log patrols.

LIVING PLANTS. Green wood may not be gathered from the forest for fires or any other purpose (it doesn't burn well, anyway). Plants may not be dug nor flowers picked.

VEHICLES. Motorized vehicles or bicycles are prohibited on service roads and trails. Observe posted speed limits on public roads within the parks.

BOATS. In the moorage area of the marine state parks the boat speed limit is 3 m.p.h. (no-wake speed). In addition to being extremely annoying to other boaters, hotrodding or racing, even in small outboard-powered dinghys, can create a wake which may swamp other small craft, send hot food flying from a cruiser's galley range, or cause other damage. Boaters are responsible for any damage caused by their wakes.

MOORAGE. Buoys and floats are on a first-come, first-served basis. The practice of individuals attempting to "reserve" space by tying a dinghy to a float

State Park mooring buoy

or buoy is not legal in the state parks. Moorage on floats or buoys is limited to 36 consecutive hours (or 2 nights).

It is courteous to use the minimum moorage space possible on a float. Beach small boats whenever able, instead of tying up to a float. Berth small cruisers or runabouts as far forward as possible, leaving the end of the float for larger boats which require deeper water and more maneuvering space.

During the busy summer season, it is considerate (and often more fun) to raft together with a friend on a buoy, thus freeing a moorage for another boater. However, this practice should be used with care during bad weather, as too many boats rafted together can displace a buoy.

When anchoring, be sure that your hook is properly set and you are not drifting, and that the swing of your anchorage will not permit you to collide with others. While artists may paint pretty pictures of harbors with boats all neatly swinging in unison, in real life it doesn't always work that way, as the shape of the hull greatly affects the way wind and tide push the boat, and the maximum northerly swing of one boat may coincide with the maximum southerly swing of another. Be sure your anchorage is secure before leaving your boat or retiring for the evening, or the "things that go bump in the night" may be you.

PETS. Pets must be on a leash no longer than eight feet and under control at all times. Some boat-bound yachtsmen regard the land facilities of the state parks merely as handy places to allow their dogs to relieve themselves. Even the most devout of animal lovers finds it hard to think kindly of these pets while trying to scrape doggie droppings from the grooves of their Topsiders. Out of courtesy for those who do wish to enjoy the shoreside attractions, remove your dog's feces from docks, walkways, trails and campgrounds.

FEES. Deception Pass, Moran and Spencer Spit State Parks charge a fee for the use of campsites. At present there is no fee for camping or use of the moorage facilities at the marine state parks which are accessible by boat only.

NOISE. Since sounds carry greater distances over water, use care that radios or boisterous noises do not penetrate to nearby boats or campsites.

VANDALISM. It probably does little good to talk about intentional vandalism here. The damaging or removal of park property is, of course, illegal and when observed should be reported to the proper authorities.

Some acts of vandalism, however, are committed out of thoughtlessness or ignorance. Spray painting or scratching graffiti on rocks or other natural features may not be recognized by park visitors as vandalism until they are confronted with a lovely sandstone wall turned ugly with mindless scrawling. Such defacement is prohibited in all parks.

Digging in the banks with shovels, picks or any similar tool is also prohibited. Holes dug in beaches for clams or for any other purpose must be filled in.

MARINE LIFE. Observe State Department of Fisheries regulations on the taking of fish and shellfish in saltwater areas; in freshwater lakes the regulations of the State Department of Game apply. It is unlawful to remove from state park beaches any living animals such as starfish, sand dollars or sea anemones, except those edible varieties defined and regulated by the State Department of Fisheries.

WILDLIFE. Hunting or harassing of wildlife and discharge of firearms is prohibited within the state parks.

EMERGENCIES OR COMPLAINTS. In parks where rangers are not on duty, the proper authority can be reached by marine or Citizen's Band radio if immediate action is necessary. A list of park rangers, their addresses, and their radio call numbers is included in the Emergency section at the back of this book. In matters of less urgency, the rangers should be contacted later by telephone or in writing.

PUBLIC TIDELANDS—WHERE, OH WHERE ARE THEY?

Large sections of the tidelands in the San Juans are state owned and are open to public recreation. These public beaches include the sea bed and shores from the line of extreme low water to the line of mean high water, even though upland property is privately owned. This is not true of all lands, for until 1969 property owners were permitted to purchase abutting tide lands from the state, and many did so.

The State Department of Natural Resources has attempted to locate and identify all public beaches throughout the state, utilizing an on-site marking system. Unfortunately, in the initial program such a large number of beach markers were destroyed by vandalism or natural causes that the marking project was abandoned.

Present plans are to identify public beaches in brochures available from the DNR, although it is not expected that the brochure covering San Juan beaches will be available until 1980 or after. When available, it can be obtained from the Department of Natural Resources, Division of Marine Land Management, Olympia, Washington, 98504.

A few of these public beaches are mentioned in this book, however it is impossible to locate them without very detailed maps of the shoreline. Until such time as the DNR is able to clearly identify these areas, beach users run a serious risk of trespassing on private property. Remember—simply because a beach is not posted as private, do not assume that it is public.

WHAT'S A WILDERNESS AREA DOING IN THE MIDDLE OF A TOURIST PARADISE?

Well, to put it bluntly, the wilderness was here first! Before the coming of man, birds nested throughout the San Juans and raised their young here, while migratory birds used the islands as resting stops. Seals and sea lions hauled out on rocks and foraged the waters. Then civilization began encroaching on the most desirable of the islands, leaving only remote offshore rocks for these timorous creatures.

Anticipating man's insatiable demands for home and recreational sites, eighty-four of these islands have been set aside as the San Juan National Wildlife Refuge and the San Juan Wilderness, providing sanctuaries for pelagic birds and animals. The U.S. Fish and Wildlife Service, which administers these sanctuaries, recognizes that safeguarding of such lands enhances the human benefits associated with wildlife and their environment.

The history of the wilderness area goes back to 1914, when Smith and Minor Islands, located in the Straits of Juan de Fuca, were first designated as wildlife refuges. Jones and Matia Islands became refuges in 1937, and in 1960 Turn Island, Bird Rocks (in Rosario Strait), Williamson Rocks (west of Fidalgo Island), Colville Island (south of Lopez Island) and Bare Island (north of Waldron Island) were established as a collective San Juan National Wildlife Refuge, with a total of 52 acres of land. Since that time other islands have been added as refuges, and in the 1970s, 79 of them (excluding Turn, Jones, Smith and Minor Islands, and five acres on Matia Island), achieved wilderness status. Jones, Turn and the Matia area remain as National Wildlife Refuges, permitting some recreational use. These protected lands today total 646 acres and range in character from barren reefs, submerged at high tide to inhospitable offshore rocks, to wooded islets, supporting deer, raccoon, fox, rabbits, river otters, weasels and other small mammals, as well as birds and seals.

At present, Jones, Turn and the five acres on Matia are managed cooperatively with the Washington State Parks and Recreation Commission as joint state parks and wildlife refuges. It is possible that in the future Jones Island will be completely taken over as a state park. In these three areas public recreation is permitted within the limitations of state park regulations. In addition, the public is urged to use special care to avoid disturbing wildlife, especially nesting birds.

As stated in the public use policy statement for the San Juan Wilderness, which was adopted in 1979, going ashore on any of the islands of the wilderness area at any time is prohibited in order to protect the wildlife there. Special permission may be granted in the case of scientific research. Such permission must be obtained from the Refuge Manager of the Nisqually National Wildlife Refuge, 2625 Parkmont Lane, Building A-2, Olympia, Washington, 98502.

TABLE OF CONTENTS

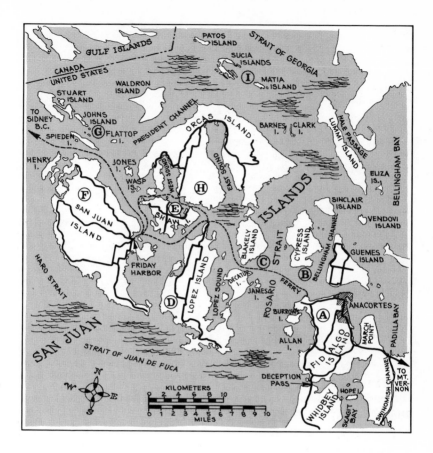

Telephoto of Padilla Bay and Mt. Baker from Cap Sante Park; Hat Island on right

A.   FIDALGO ISLAND

Fidalgo seems barely an island at all, lying so close that bridges bind it to the mainland, providing easy access to all of civilization's conveniences. Yet it has the island advantages of miles and miles of shoreline, with beaches and bays to suit every prupose, and that sense of unique character that only true physical separation, and not political boundaries, can create.

Fidalgo is divided into three distinct sections, or "lobes"—in fact with an extraordinary high tide it could become three separate islands. The eastern lobe, bordered on the east by the Swinomish Channel and on the west by Skagit and Similk Bays is almost entirely the Swinomish Indian Reservation. Waterfront property on the west shore and at Shelter Bay on the southeastern tip, is leased to non-Indians by the tribe for homes and vacation cottages. The sparsely settled heavily forested interior is selectively logged.

The long amoebe-like foot of March Point, extending into the tide flats of Fidalgo and Padilla Bay, comprises most of the middle section of the island. Huge storage tanks, factories and stacks of oil refineries on the point seem strange bedfellows to the small farms dotting the surrounding lands. Although the refineries, the pipelines and the steady parade of oil tankers make environmentalists queasy, refinery jobs and the associated economic boom is generally welcomed by Fidalgo Islanders, and the refineries have remained environmentally "clean"—so far.

The western lobe of the island, its largest section, displays the true "San Juan" character, with rugged shoreline, glacier-scrubbed granite domes and pocket lakes nestled in green forest. Here, in its several public parks, visitors can explore beaches and bluffs to their heart's content, and look out to the enticing shores and waters of myriad more islands.

Fidalgo Island is reached by following Highway 20 west from the 230 exit on I-5, just north of Mt. Vernon, for 8½ miles (13½ km). After crossing the channel onto Fidalgo Island, Highway 20 splits at Sharpes Corner at the end of Fidalgo Bay, 3¼ miles (5 km) from the bridges. Both branches of the Y are still Highway 20—the right leg goes north for 2½ more miles (6½ km) to Anacortes, while the left branch heads southwest, reaching Deception Pass State Park in 4½ miles (7¼ km).

The bridge over the Swinomish Channel at La Conner also crosses to the island, connecting with roads up the center and on the west shore of the Indian reservation.

The island can be reached from the south by taking the Mukilteo ferry to Columbia Beach on Whidbey Island and driving north on Highway 525, which becomes Highway 20 midway, for a distance of 50 miles (80 km) to the Deception Pass bridge. Bicyclists often leave their four wheels at the Mukilteo ferry landing and transfer to two wheels for a long, scenic ride through Whidbey countryside. The Keystone ferry from Port Townsend to Whidbey Island provides access to the island from the Olympic Peninsula.

Fidalgo Island's two unique waterways, the Swinomish Channel and Deception Pass, serve as boating portals to the San Juans and Canadian Gulf Islands for hordes of pleasure vessels traveling up Saratoga Passage from Puget Sound. The southern entrance to Swinomish Channel is about 50 nautical miles from Shilshole Bay in Seattle, while Deception Pass is 6 nautical miles farther.

SWINOMISH CHANNEL

Area: 5½ nautical miles in length, 10 nautical miles from channel entrance to channel exit
Access: Boat or car
Facilities (at La Conner): Groceries, stores, fuel, marine repair, boat launching, transient moorage on docks with electrical hookups and water, restrooms, showers, restaurants, hotels
Attractions: Boating, canoeing, fishing, sightseeing, shopping, hiking

Fidalgo makes the grade to island status by virtue of the Swinomish Channel, a 60-foot-wide waterway which separates it from the Skagit mainland. Named the Swinomish Slough on old maps, the canal is dredged throughout to a depth of 8 feet, and both entrances are well marked with navigational devices for the use of commercial and recreational boaters seeking to avoid the turbulent waters of Deception Pass.

A. FIDALGO ISLAND

A trip on the channel is reminiscent of European canal boating, cruising slowly by farms, homes and a village, waving cheerily to the "natives" on shore and to fellow-boaters. It is truly a unique experience for Northwesterners.

When approaching the Swinomish Channel from either end, even small boats should have on hand a good navigational chart and follow it closely, for only the marked channel is dredged and all the surrounding area is tide flat where in places even a canoe can run aground. Do not be tempted to cut the corner into innocent-looking water, but follow the channel clear out to its end, or you may spend a tide change on the mud flat.

The southern entrance, known as Hole in the Wall, is a dog-leg run between the 100-foot vertical walls of two rock knobs. A lovely spot, but no fun in a fog. From here the canal straightens out to gently meander through Skagit flatland, edged by levees.

Once in the channel, skippers can breathe more easily and enjoy the trip, however they should stay near the middle, for the sides can be quite shoal; pass approaching boats port-to-port and maintain a no-wake speed.

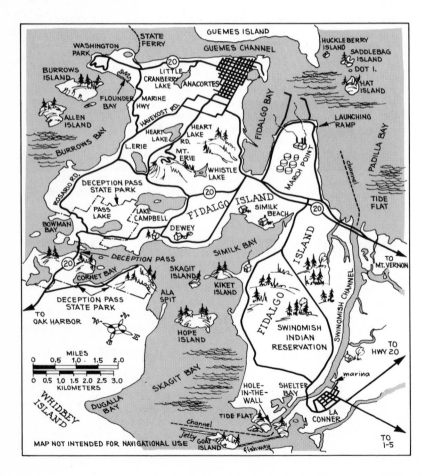

Swinomish Channel from the Rainbow Bridge at La Conner

A mile north of Hole in the Wall, La Conner is the quintessential little seaside tourist village, with waterfront businesses built on pilings edging the canal. Founded in 1867, it was a center of commerce during the time of steamboat traffic on Puget Sound; many of the town's buildings are listed in the National Register of Historic Places. Today it is an artists colony and tourist center with interesting shops, restaurants, museums and historical sites.

On the west shore of the canal are the Swinomish Indian boat docks, fish cannery and (as of summer, 1979), the Swinomish Market which offers fresh seafood, barbecued salmon and Indian crafts for sale to visitors. Docking and moorage are provided near the building.

Floats along the waterfront invite temporary moorage by visiting boats. Overnight berths are provided by the Port of Skagit County, which operates two yacht basins just north of town.

Trailered boats and canoes may be launched in La Conner at a public ramp north of the Rainbow Bridge. To reach it, follow Chilberg Road into La Conner; just past the Pioneer Monument turn left onto Maple, then right on Caldonia, left on 2nd and right on Sherman to the waterfront. An ample parking area adjoins the ramp.

Since the waterway connects two large bodies of saltwater (Skagit Bay on the south and Padilla Bay on the north), water flows inward at both ends of the channel during a flood tide and outward during the ebb. The precise location of the transition is hard to predict, however general knowledge of the forecasted tides can be very useful to canoeists and boaters in small craft.

While the run through the channel is fun in a large baot, it can be enchanting in a small one, with side trips up narrow sloughs and eye-to-eye encounters with

Black Brandt geese

great blue herons, ducks and other marsh birds. During the winter many of the birds common to the Skagit Game Range a few miles to the south—whistling swans, snow geese, Brandt, gulls, ducks and terns—may also be seen here from the water or from roads and trails along the levees.

MARCH POINT AND PADILLA BAY

Facilities: Boat launch
Attractions: Boating, canoeing, fishing, clams, crabs, bird watching

The smooth mass of March Point rises out of the ooze of surrounding tide flats bearing a heavy load of silvery oil storage tanks. Two long, slender piers extend outward for over ½ mile like antennas of a trilobite, reaching out to Guemes Channel. The physical analogy to a giant, creeping insect is appropriate, for there are those who fear its refineries herald encroaching industrialism in the Skagit and San Juans.

Although its heartland is given over to commercialism, timid shorebirds still skitter along the shores of March Point and rafts of migratory waterfowl still gather in the adjacent bays. Good birdwatching from beach or canoe in fall and winter.

Padilla Bay hosts the state's only large wintering population of Brant. These small geese with a particular palate dine almost exclusively on eelgrass and sea lettuce found in huge beds in the brackish water of the bay. In spring they depart, flying in wavering lines, for nesting grounds in the Arctic.

To reach the shoreline road around March Point from Highway 20, ½ mile (¾ km) after crossing the bridge over the Swinomish Channel turn right onto March Point Road. The blacktopped road circles around the point for about 7 miles (11 km), returning to Highway 20 at a junction at the head of Fidalgo Bay. Stopping places along the road are few.

The northern section of the eastern shore is a public recreation area with clams and crabs to be found in the tide flat, and fine fishing just offshore. A public boat launching ramp with a large parking lot is located near the tip of the point; more parking is found a little farther along, around the point. RV camping is permitted in the parking areas. Boats launched here frequently head for Saddlebag Island State Park, 2½ nautical miles to the north, or to the popular salmon fishing grounds just off nearby Hat Island.

Small boats can spend a pleasant afternoon along the shoreline and in the serene waters of the huge, shallow bay. Bayview State Park lies 3 nautical miles to the east on the far shore of the bay. Use care, for the majority of the bay is less than 2 feet (½ meter) deep at mean lower low water; explore on a rising tide so that incoming water can float you off if you become grounded.

SADDLEBAG ISLAND STATE PARK

Park area: 23 acres
Access: Boat only
Facilities: Campsites, picnic tables, fireplaces, pit toilets, *no water*
Attractions: Fishing, crabs, scuba diving, hiking

Conveniently located near the mouth of Padilla Bay, and only 2 nautical miles northeast of Anacortes, Saddlebag Island State Park is heavily used by boaters who drop by for the day to try their hand at crabbing and fishing, and by those who use its coves as handy anchorages on their way to somewhere else. For those visitors who take the time to go ashore, the trails which circle the island's grassy bluffs give boaters a chance to steady their sea legs and enjoy bird's eye views of the activity below—salmon fishing boats drifting offshore, patiently awaiting a strike: behemoth tankers, escorted by stubby tugs, heading for the oil refinery at March Point; sailboats with bright spinnakers looking like flowers blowing in the wind.

Saddlebag Island is cast in the familiar San Juan pattern of two rocky, scrub-covered headlands joined by a low, narrow neck, thus forming a pair of coves on either side of the landmass, and creating the outline which inspired this island's name. In this case the coves face north and south, with the one on the north being slightly larger and more deeply indented.

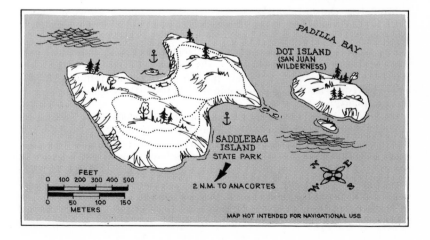

Northern cove at Saddlebag Island State Park

The water east of the island is extremely shallow; approach from the west, especially during a minus tide. There are no mooring buoys at the park, however several good anchorages are available, the best being in the northern cove. The southern cove is shallower with a thick growth of eelgrass, making it difficult for anchors to dig in.

A small camp area is at the head of the bay on the north, with pit toilets located along the trail which crosses the middle of the island. The southern bay has a picnic table on the beach, however it is for day use only, as there is not enough space for tenting on the narrow, driftwood-choked beach.

Saddlebag, Dot and Hat Islands are perched on the edge of a huge submarine shelf; to the east the water is less than a fathom in depth, while immediately to the west the shelf plummets to a depth of 30-40 fathoms. The rich variety of marine organisms living on the long flat and on the steep walls of the shelf make this a feeding area for sea birds, fish, crabs and even the local river otters. The Hat Island vicinity is an extremely popular sport salmon fishing spot, and Saddlebag Island has a reputation as one of the best sport crab harvesting areas in the San Juans.

Unfortunately crab thieves have become a problem at Saddlebag, as well as in other crabbing areas. In many cases the pirates merely remove the night's catch from a trap, however they have been known to abscound with crabs, trap, line, floats and all. Although some angered victims have blamed this thievery on commercial crabbers who resent the competition of sportsmen, it is far more likely that the thieves are other "sportsmen" unwilling to invest in the equipment and to spend the time to catch their own food.

Smaller Dot Island, just a stone's throw away, is a bird nesting area and animal refuge of the San Juan Islands Wilderness.

ANACORTES

Access: Car, boat or airplane
Facilities (in downtown Anacortes and at Flounder Bay): Groceries, stores,
  fuel, marine repair, boat launching, boat rentals and charters, transient
  moorage on docks with water and electrical hookups, restaurants,
  restrooms, laundry, showers, scuba shop, hotels. (At ferry terminal): U.S.
  Customs
Attractions: Boating, fishing, scuba diving, hiking, sightseeing, shopping

When Amos Bowman first arrived at Fidalgo Island in 1876, he came to the
conclusion that Ship Harbor, on the northern tip of the island, with its fine, deep
harbor and strategic location at the entrance to Puget Sound, was perfectly
suited as a site for a major seaport. He purchased 186 acres of land, convinced
other settlers of the merits of the island, and founded a town, naming it
Anacortes after his wife, Anna Curtis Bowman.

All that was needed to assure its future as "the New York of the Pacific Coast"
was a railroad to provide connecting land transportation for the impending rush
of people and goods. It was a time of feverish financial speculation—five different railway depots were built at locations around the island, each one expecting
to be the Northwest's connection to the Orient.

When the Northern Pacific finally completed its first set of transcontinental
rails to western Washington, alas, its terminus was in Tacoma, not in Anacortes
as Bowman had been led to expect. Instead of unloading at the wharf already
constructed and awaiting cargoes at Ship Harbor, ships headed down-sound to
Commencement Bay. The anticipated boom fizzled.

The great westward expansion did benefit Anacortes, of course, although in a
more modest way than had been hoped. Railroad spurs eventually came up the

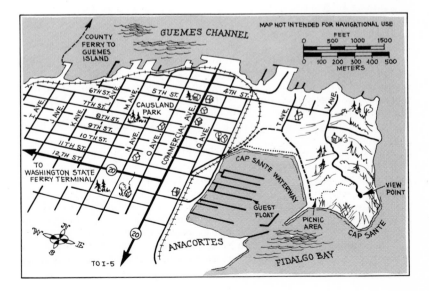

Anacortes from Cap Sante Park

sound and canneries, sawmills, shipyards and other industry brought steady growth to the area, however none inspired the boom that early entrepreneurs had prophesied.

Perhaps the failure of those early city fathers eventually became a triumph; reflecting on the industrial sprawl and pollution attendant to Tacoma today, and imagining all of that transplanted to Anacortes, one can only shudder at what the San Juans might be if Amos Bowman had fully realized his dream.

Today the city serves as the portal to the San Juans, with its state ferry transporting nearly ¾ million tourists and residents to the islands annually, and its marinas chartering boats and offering marine services to thousands more.

The Washington State ferries provide service from Anacortes to Lopez, Shaw, Orcas and San Juan Islands, and Sidney, B.C. To reach the terminal at Shannon Point, follow Highway 20 into Anacortes, where it joins Commercial Ave. and then turns left on 12th Ave.; follow signs from here to the ferry landing. For a more detailed discussion regarding use of the ferries see the introduction to this book.

For tourists arriving on their own boat, or planning to charter one, marinas are located around the saltwater perimeter of the city at Flounder Bay on the southwest, or closer to the center of town on Guemes Channel and behind the protective headland of Cap Sante.

A marina on Flounder Bay is a favorite stopover for pleasure boaters who are traveling through Deception Pass. Although it is 4 miles (6½ km) from the city center, the marina and nearby shops can meet most boating needs.

Cap Sante Boat Haven, on Cap Sante Waterway, is operated by the Port of Anacortes to provide moorages and facilities for transient boaters. The fine restaurants and stores of Anacortes are only a few blocks' walk from the docks.

All of the marinas have launching facilities. Public boat ramps for trailer boats are located at Sunset Beach in Washington Park and at March Point.

Private airplanes may land at the municipal airport on the west side of town, ½ mile from the ferry terminal, or the local air service can be chartered for flights to the islands.

Many tourists hurry through the city, on their way to distant islands, not realizing that Anacortes itself has beaches, bays, viewpoints and natural treasures to rival those found on the other San Juans.

It has perhaps the finest parks of any city of similar size in the state, ranging from carefully-groomed, pocket-sized Causland Park, to Washington Park, with its rugged bluffs beautified by time and weather. Mt. Erie is unique—a city park which does not even lie within the boundaries of the city.

CAUSLAND PARK

If the boat crew is ready to mutiny after the days of confinement aboard, an 8-block stroll and a picnic at Causland Memorial Park may be in order. From Cap Sante Waterway walk west about 4 blocks to N Avenue, then north 4 more blocks to 8th. The 1-block park, with its closely-trimmed lawns, and long walls and band shell of intricate stone mosaic is a small delight. Picnic tables to boot!

Across the street to the west, at 8th and M, is the Museum of History, containing momentos of pioneer days on Fidalgo Island (open Sunday and Wednesday afternoons). Round trip from the harbor and back is about 1½ miles (2½ km).

CAP SANTE CITY PARK

An imposing rocky headland rising 200 feet above the marinas of Anacortes provides breathtaking views of Fidalgo Island, March Point, Hat and Saddlebag Islands, and Mt. Baker reigning over all.

To reach the park from Anacortes, drive north on Commercial Avenue, and turn right on 4th. Continue on 4th to its end and turn right on V Avenue, following the winding road uphill to a large parking lot atop the rock monolith.

A picnic area at the base of the rock can be reached by turning south off 4th onto T Avenue and following it past private residences to its end by a rock jetty. Several picnic tables are on grassy promontories overlooking the harbor. A crude trail leads through timber up the hillside to the top of the cape.

The viewpoint is a challenging hike from Cap Sante marinas. Follow Q north to 9th and turn right onto the gravel road which circles the head of the bay to the picnic area and the trail to the top of the headland. Total distance to top of Cap Sante about 1 mile (1½ km), elevation gain 195 feet (60 meters).

The rolling grassy hillsides on the west side of the cape can be descended with care, but they are certain to give mothers of small children cardiac arrest, for they seem to drop quite abruptly to the water. The south and east slopes are glacier-polished granite, broken by patchy grass. Midway down, a row of iron posts marks the point where the "rather steep" becomes "extremely steep" (and dangerous). End your exploration here.

Little Cranberry Lake

LITTLE CRANBERRY LAKE

What can be so special about 25 acres of shallow water choked with reeds and grass and drowned timber? Linger there awhile, and perhaps you'll understand. Little Cranberry Lake is another of Anacortes' city parks; this one has only nominal developments—a few picnic tables and a narrow trail, but that seems quite ample for this humble pond.

To reach the lake from Anacortes, drive west on Highway 20, which merges into Sunset Avenue. About 1½ miles (2½ km) before reaching the side road leading to the ferry terminal, turn left (south) onto Georgia St. Drive for three blocks through a new housing subdivision; as the street turns right and begins to climb it deteriorates into a narrow dirt road. The lakeshore parking lot is reached in about ½ mile (¾ km).

In timber to the east, beyond the concrete dam, is a primitive camping area with picnic tables and fireplaces. At times trail motorcycles razz around through the campground; between their abuse and heavy use by campers, the area is a barren dust (or mud) flat. Fortunately the difficulty of the shore trail prevents bikers from spreading their destruction completely around the lake.

Open to fishing year around, the lake is a fine spot for bass, perch and catfish. Boats with motors are not permitted. The maze-like bogs invite exploration with canoe or pram. At the southern end of the lake silvered trunks of drowned trees form a ghostly forest, and fallen timber supports growths of thick grass and tiny new trees, as Nature proceeds with its continuous recycling.

The trail around the lake has been brushed out by Anacortes civic groups. At times confusing side trails make the route difficult to follow, but generally the correct route lies quite near the shore, avoiding those which branch away from it. At the south end of the lake is a "fat man's misery", where a ten-foot high rock sits smack on the lakeshore and the trail has been built out just enough to enable a hiker to squeeze by. Total distance around the lake is about 1¾ miles (2¾ km).

Life teems in the marsh environment. Watch quietly at the edge of shallow pools and you may see the silvery flash of darting fish, frogs swiftly kicking by, followed by a trail of bubbles, or menacing crayfish lurking among the rocks. Great blue herons stalk the ponds, spearing prey with their long bills. In spring watch for song birds, mating and building nests, while in winter waterfowl pause on their migratory way.

WASHINGTON PARK

Park Area: 220 acres
Access: Car or boat
Facilities: Campsites, picnic tables. fireplaces, water at Sunset Beach and in
    the campground only, restrooms, showers, picnic area, shelters,
    playground, boat launching ramp (fee)
Attractions: Boating, hiking, viewpoints, scuba diving

Undoubtedly the crowning glory of the Anacortes city parks system, Washington Park has 220 acres of forest and beach and panoramic viewpoints. In addition to the steady flow of auto-bound sightseers, many others wisely choose to use the park for road walking, jogging or cycling, traveling slowly enough to fully soak in its beauty.

To reach the park by car or bicycle from Anacortes, follow signs on Highway 20 west toward the San Juan ferry landing. When the highway turns downhill to the ferry terminal, bear left instead for ¾ mile (1 km) to the park entrance. A bicycle lane is provided along the left side of the road much of the way.

Immediately to the right of the entrance is Sunset Beach, where a large picnic area and the boat launching ramp are located. For visitors arriving by boat, Sunset Bay is the only possible landing spot in the park; boats must be beached or anchored out in the bay, as the short finger pier adjacent the ramp is for loading purposes only. Boaters may also reach the park by walking the road from the marina on Flounder Bay to the park entrance, a distance of ¾ mile (1 km).

A few feet beyond the boat launching road at Sunset Beach is the campground, with forty-eight pleasant sites separated by timber and undergrowth, open year around (fee).

A. FIDALGO ISLAND

From here the route and mode of transportation are up to the visitor. Pedestrians may choose to walk the road from towering sea-level forest upward to grassy wind-swept knolls and glacier-scoured rocks 200 feet above Burrows Pass. or hike the rocky beach from Sunset Bay westward until tide and the steepening bluffs of Fidalgo Head force the route inland. The road can be avoided almost entirely by following forest paths near the edge of the bluff from West Beach all the way to the Havekost Memorial. Loop trip is about 3 miles (4¾ km), longer if enticing side trails are explored; elevation gain is 260 feet (80 meters).

Whether traveling by trail or road, West Beach is an inviting wayside stop. At Green Point is a pull-out with parking space for a number of cars and an interesting log shelter. Picnic tables on the grassy point have balcony views of boating and ferry traffic in Guemes Channel, with backdrops of Cypress, Guemes and distant islands.

A wooden staircase leads down to the shore where waves from Rosario Strait toss driftwood logs onto the narrow, bedrock beach. South, beyond Fidalgo Head can be seen a lighthouse situated high on a bluff on Burrows Island. This side of the park is a favorite with scuba divers experienced enough to handle the strong current and deep water.

Uprising cliffs of Fidalgo Head prevent a complete beach circuit of the park; however, the shoreline on the south side can be reached by carefully working down the steep grassy slopes from the road viewpoints above. The bluffs drop off abruptly, so there are no beaches, but the tawny grass sprinkled with wildflowers, the weather-twisted trees and the briny view more than compensate.

As the road makes its final loop before heading back down to the park entrance, the last viewpoint features a small marble monument to T. H. Havekost, who bequeathed the land for this park to the city of Anacortes. Havekost was a pioneer industrialist and land speculator on Fidalgo Island in the late 1800s. He purchased land in the area expecting, like many others, that

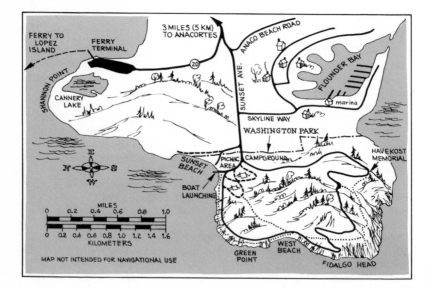

Burrows Bay from Washington Park; Burrows Island on left, Mt. Erie in distance

Burrows Bay would be the terminus of the new railroad. We can be grateful to him that when the railroad failed to materialize he saved this lovely corner of the island for the enjoyment of all.

BURROWS AND ALLAN ISLANDS

Lifting green forested shoulders from the waters of Burrows Bay, Burrows and Allan Islands may seem to be every man's dream of an island hideaway, however the very rugged nature that gives the islands their beauty, coupled with the lack of water, has served to limit settlement on these shores.

Spanish explorers named them "Las dos islas Morrows"—Two Islands of the Forts, and truly with their steep slopes they are fortress-like. Mountainous Burrows Island, rising abruptly to a height of 650 feet, is often admired from promontories at Washington Park. Against the mass of the island backdrop, boats in the channel below seem almost to be toys.

Boaters attempting to run between Young and Burrows Islands should be wary of a large rock which lies in the middle of the channel. A rocky shelf extends out from the south side of Allen Island; use care approaching this shore.

Small bays around the two islands serve as pleasant fair-weather lunch stops, however all shorelands are private, with the exception of the western point of Burrows. Here, at the site of the lighthouse, the State Parks and Recreation Commission has recently acquired 40½ acres of surplused government property, unneeded now that the light is automated. Plans are to develop a limited recreational boating facility on the beach, however as of 1979 no improvements were completed.

35

FIDALGO HEARTLAND

MT. ERIE

No discussion of the San Juans can be complete without mention of Mt. Erie, for it is an orientation point visible throughout the islands. Its distinctive silhouette, with its abruptly rising south face, is unmistakable. How many conversations from boat or ferry or viewpoint begin: "There's Mt. Erie, so Deception Pass is about there, and. . . "

And how many people, having seen the mountain from afar so many times have ever gone to the mountain to see where they've been? Well, probably quite a few, for on summer days the parking lot is jammed with cars, motorcycles and even tour busses, and the mountaintop is filled with sightseers and picnickers and photographers and mountain climbers and hikers and what-have-you. So at such times it's not a place for solitude, nor to silently contemplate the deeper meaning of life while surrounded by Nature's great works.

However not even elbow-to-elbow people can dim the glory of the view. The panorama spreads for nearly 250 miles, from Mt. Rainier on the south to Mt. Garibaldi in Canada on the north. To the east are the Cascades, with Mt. Baker rising above them; westward are San Juan Islands of velvet green, dotting the blue sea.

To reach Mt. Erie from I-5, follow signs on Highway 20 toward Deception Pass. At the Y at the east end of Campbell Lake, take the right hand fork; drive for 1½ miles (2½ km) to another Y and bear right again. As the road curves around the foot of Mt. Erie, watch for a short pull-off loop on the right.

To drive to the mountain from Anacortes, the Heart Lake Road can be followed south from H Avenue to the pull-off loop described above, immediately south of Heart Lake.

Ray Auld Drive, a blacktopped road, begins at the back of the pull-off loop and twists up the mountainside for 2 miles (3 km) to the summit.

Paths lace the 1,300-foot mountaintop. Concrete steps near the abandoned radar installation lead to a small observation platform with an iron railing for viewers with vertigo. Experienced hikers can work their way downward over the mossy slopes, but use care; many paths dead end in dangerous cliffs. Mountain climbing classes frequently spend the day here practicing rock climbing and rapelling techniques; recently the park has also become popular with hang gliding enthusiasts.

Mt. Erie is an Anacortes City Park, purchased and donated to the city by the local Kiwanas Club. The winding mountain road was the labor of love of Ray Auld, a Fidalgo Island resident who worked for 20 years, clearing and transplanting natural vegetation, to make it the most beautiful drive in the county—a drive to match the view at the top.

FIDALGO LAKES

From the summit of Mt. Erie, a number of lakes can be seen scattered across the Fidalgo landscape. Whistle Lake, lying east of the mountain is a water reservoir for the city of Anacortes. Other, smaller ponds are on private property, however three of the large lakes have developed public accesses for use by boaters and fishermen.

Campbell Lake from Mt. Erie; Hope and Skagit Islands on the left, Skagit Bay in the distance

This trio of lakes offer good quiet-water paddling for canoeists, although boats with motors are permitted on them, and at times they are heavily used. When outboards shatter the peace, canoeists may well choose to retreat to other, calmer waters.

Campbell Lake. The largest and most srikingly beautiful of the Fidalgo Island lakes. with bucolic green pastures rolling down to the lakeshore and a toy-like island in its center. The public access and boat launching ramp are on the north shore; watch for a signed side road about ¾ mile (1 km) west of the Highway 20-Campbell Lake Road intersection.

The banks of the island are quite steep; however, at two places landing is possible for onshore exploration. The waters hold largemouth bass, perch and catfish, and are open to fishing year around.

Lake Erie. This lily-pad bordered lake offers good fishing for rainbow trout, or just pleasant paddling while enjoying the view of the steep face of Mt. Erie, and, at times, of hang glider pilots launching their craft from the summit.

The public access is on the southeast end of the lake; turn left at the second Y at the east end of the lake. Watch for an obscure side road on the right in less than ½ mile (¾ km).

Heart Lake. Not as spectacular as the other two lakes, but an ultramarine gem nonetheless. Marsh birds twitter and scold in the cattails; a sudden splash of water gives evidence of a hungry trout, or perhaps only a frog. Pink water lilies on the lake were planted many years ago by Ray Auld.

Lands surrounding the lake are all state or city owned, thus the boggy shoreline remains natural. The lake is not always tranquil, however, for at times it is used to race small hydros. The public launching area is on the northeast side of the heart-shaped lake, just north of the point where the Heart Lake Road parallels the road.

Deception Pass bridge

Deception Pass State Park

Park Area: 2,339 acres
Access: Car or boat
Facilities: Extensive camping, picnicking, and boating accommodations —
   refer to specific areas
Attractions: Hiking, boating, canoeing, swimming, scuba and free diving,
   beachcombing, fishing (freshwater and saltwater), sightseeing

With its generous samplings of all the treasures created when land meets sea, Deception Pass serves as a perfect introduction to the San Juan Islands. Here are quiet virgin forests; coves and bays and wave-tossed beaches holding treasures from the sea; grassy bluffs festooned with twisted "bonsai" trees and bright meadow flowers; awesome rock escarpments; lakes hosting trout and waterfowl; deer, seals, otters, eagles and bizarre marine life—all to be enjoyed by motorist, bicyclist, pedestrian or mariner.

Although some purists would contend with a haughtly sniff that Deception Pass is not part of the San Juans, in reality the separation of the islands to the west is purely political, dictated by county boundaries for bureaucratic convenience, for the geological and historical kniship is undeniable.

The same strata of Late Jurassic igneous rock which underlies Turtleback Mountain on Orcas Island forms the enclosing granite walls of Deception Pass. The Pleistocene glacier which rasped its way across Orcas and San Juan and Lopez Islands just 15,000 years ago, also gouged out the bays and channels of Deception Pass and smoothed the brows of Bowman Hill, Goose Rock and Mt. Erie. The first explorers who charted the islands noted the relationships of these islands and their network of waterways and designated the entire area as "the San Juan Archipeligo".

So enrapturing are the physical beauties of the park, that many visitors never realize that the area is equally interesting historically. The territory from Deception Pass eastward belonged to the Indians of the Swinomish tribe, who harvested the vast runs of salmon which swarmed through the channels. The pass obviously impressed early Indians as much as it does people today, for it is mentioned in several of their legends; one tells of an Indian princess who lived at Deception Pass, and who became the bride of the king of the fishes, going to live with him in his underwater kingdom. Her long, flowing hair, turned green from exposure to water, can still be seen drifting in the current, although some people know it only is seaweed.

Pioneer history of the Deception Pass area was colorful, sometimes even lurid—replete with tales of hardy pioneers who settled the land, and some equally hardy smugglers, cutthroats and pirates who sought greater fortune, or perhaps just greater adventure.

During the late 1800s, a portion of the land within the present park was designated as a military reservation for the coastal defense of the region. At the outbreak of World War I, when all of Puget Sound bristled with cannon aimed seaward, three 3-inch guns were brought from Fort Casey on the southern end of Whidbey Island and set up at North Beach, and a searchlight was installed at West Point.

At the end of the war, local residents began a movement to have the area, already a favorite picknicking, camping and rhododendron-viewing spot, officially

A. FIDALGO ISLAND

designated as a state park. In 1921, 1,746 acres were dedicated as Deception Pass State Park. Since that time additional lands have been purchased, donated or transferred to the jurisdiction of the park from other state agencies and private citizens until the present acreage is slightly in excess of 2300 acres, encompassing six entire islands (and parts of Whidbey and Fidalgo Islands), two lakes and one ocean (as the park brochure describes it.)

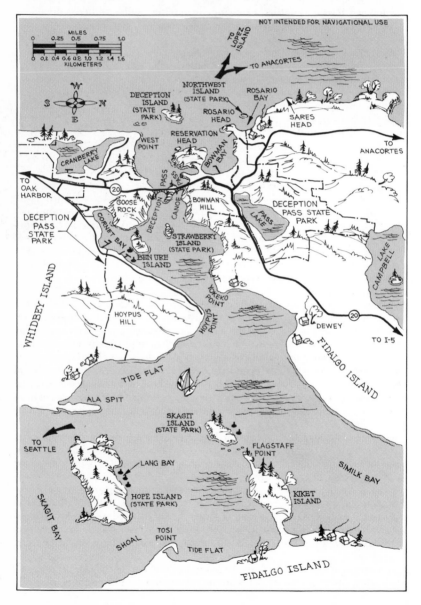

Hope Island moorage

Local residents provided the funds and labor for early development within the park. They built two bathhouses and a community kitchen and constructed access roads and trails. It was not until 1933 that a comprehensive, modern plan for the park was formulated, when the Civilian Conservation Corps began the work of clearing brush, digging wells and constructing the permanent park buildings, most of which are still in use today.

Evening fireside talks and slide shows telling of the history of the park, or describing the flora, fauna and natural features, are conducted during summer evenings near the Cranberry Lake Campground. The talks are well worth attending, as they greatly enhance the understanding and enjoyment of the park.

Deception Pass State Park can be reached by ferry from Mukilteo to Columbia Beach on the southeast tip of Whidbey Island, then by car or bicycle along Highway 525 (which becomes Highway 20), the length of the island to its northern end, a distance of 50 miles (80 km).

To approach Deception Pass by car from the north, omitting the occasionally crowded, although always scenic, ferry ride, leave I-5 at Exit 230, just north of Mount Vernon, following Highway 20 east. Signs direct the route to the park, 18 miles (29 km) from the freeway.

The mouth of Deception Pass lies just east of the confluence of the Strait of Juan de Fuca and Rosario Strait. Mariners approaching from the south often duck behind the shelter of Whidbey Island and run Saratoga Passage and Skagit Bay northward, following the channel west at Hoypus Point to reach the pass.

A. FIDALGO ISLAND

Trailered boats can be launched at Cornet Bay and Bowman Bay within the park, larger boats may rent lift facilities at Cornet Bay Marina, adjacent to the park, or Skyline Marina (which also charters boats), 6½ nautical miles to the north at Flounder Bay on Fidalgo Island.

The state park holds such a wealth of recreation and natural beauty that it has been treated in sections of three of The Mountaineers' guide books—**Trips and Trails, 1,** by E. M. Sterling describes the park for car-campers and day-trippers, Harvey Manning's **Footsore 3** guides more ambitious pedestrians, while this volume surveys the area with a largely water-oriented viewpoint. **Footsore 3** so thoroughly (and so well) describes the trails that some are only mentioned briefiy here, with a stronger emphasis on watery adventure.

Erin and Bill Woods' books, **Bicycling the Backroads around Puget Sound** and **Bicycling the Backroads of Northwest Washington,** also published by The Mountaineers, describe tours on Camano and Fidalgo Islands which include stops at the park.

HOPE AND SKAGIT ISLANDS

Island Areas: Hope Island—166 acres; Skagit Island—21 acres
Access: Boat only
Facilities: Mooring buoys, picnic tables. fireplaces, pit toilet, *no water*
Attractions: Fishing, canoeing, crabs, clams, scuba diving, beachcombing

Stretched across the middle of the channel between Whidbey and Fidalgo Islands, Hope Island heralds the end of Skagit Bay and the beginning of Deception Pass waters. Hope, and its smaller neighbor, Skagit Island, are undeveloped sections of Deception Pass State Park property.

The meager indentation of Lang Bay, on the north side of Hope Island, holds four buoys. Ashore, three picnic tables with fireplaces can be found in clearings above the beach; drinking water is not available.

During moderate-to-low tides the beach can be walked for a mile or more from Lang Bay, around the east end of the island to a magnificent sand and driftwood beach on the south. Take note of the damage that slovenly camping can do—runaway campfires on this beach have charred large sections of the beach driftwood. In addition to destroying the beauty of the beach and killing the small creatures that inhabit it, such fires also send up sparks which can ignite nearby forests, causing even greater damage.

Less than a mile to the north, Skagit Island is a much smaller version of Hope Island, duplicating its open, grassy bluffs on the southwest side and thick forest on the remainder. A 6-foot rocky bank encircles the island, except on the northwest side where a shoal reaches out to Kiket Island. Two buoys off the northeast shore provide a place to hang a boat while dinghy-exploring nearby shallow waters, or while waiting to go through the pass.

Shore adventurers can hike the trail which rings the island along the top of the embankment. On the northeast end of the island are two primitive campsites. Raccoons, porcupines, crows and other scavangers often scatter trash; to minimize the problem, burn food scraps and papers in fireplaces and take other garbage home with you. The water around the islands, east to Hoypus Point and north to the shallows of Similk Bay offer splendid small boat excursions, however

Hope Island beach

the tidal current is extremely strong in some areas and the paddle-propelled or under-powered craft may find itself going in a different direction than intended. Use care, watch for tide rips and stay well away from large, moving boats.

At the turn of the century Skagit was said to be a hideout for smugglers and all sorts of ruffians on the run from justice. Its strategic location, at the bend of the channel, with views into Deception Pass and down-channel into Skagit Bay made any furtive approach by law boats quite difficult.

CORNET BAY

Access: Car or boat
Facilities (at the state park): Dock with float, mooring buoys, boat launching (ramp), picnic tables, fireplaces, restrooms; (at Cornet Bay Marina): dock with floats, boat launching (lift), fuel, groceries, snack bar, laundry, restrooms, showers
Attractions: Fishing. boating, bicycling, scuba diving, hiking, beachcombing, clams

Just a watery mile east of Deception Pass, Cornet Bay is a placid refuge from the often-turbulent waters of the pass. For boaters planning to head east to cruise the quietude of Skagit Bay, or those waiting for slack tide to enable them to run the pass, Cornet Bay offers both launching facilities for trailer boats and mooring facilities for larger ones that arrive by sea.

To reach Cornet Bay by land, drive south across the Deception Pass bridge onto Whidbey Island and past the park headquarters at the Cranberry Lake entrance. About 1 mile (1½ km) south of the bridge, turn east onto Cornet Bay Road, the state park marine facilities are reached in 1¼ more miles (2 km).

Traffic is generally light on this road, making it an excellent bicycle detour. The blacktopped run is downhill or level all the way to road end at Hoypus Point, with a 100-foot climb back to the Highway 20 intersection on the return.

Deception Pass from Hoypus Point road

The state park dock has moorage space on a float for six to ten boats and on seven buoys in the bay. Moorage is limited to 36 hours. Good anchorages can be found across the bay near Ben Ure Island, but the head of the bay is quite shoal. Immediately adjacent the dock are boat launching ramps, finger piers for cargo loading and a large parking area.

Commercially operated Cornet Bay Marina, which is slightly farther into the bay, provides a float with overnight moorages, a launching lift and supplies.

Privately owned Ben Ure Island, lying in the mouth of Cornet Bay, was named for an Anacortes businessman-turned smuggler who lived there with his Indian wife during the late 1800s. The story goes that when planning to be away on a "business" trip, Ure would instruct his wife to build an evening campfire on the northern tip of the island. If Revenue agents were lying in wait in Cornet Bay, she would signal her husband by standing in front of the fire to block its light; if all was clear she sat to the side and its beacon would guide him home. Today a navigational light is located near the spot where Ben Ure's wife maintained her navigational aid.

Boaters unfamiliar with the area should not attempt to enter Cornet Bay on the west side of Ben Ure Island, as a shoal extends westward from the island.

HOYPUS POINT

The park road continues northeast from Cornet Bay, along the shore to Hoypus Point. A gated side road and a gravel pit which are passed are start points for a 3½-mile forest hike which loops around Hoypus Hill.

The road drive is scenic enough, with views through a fringe of trees of boating traffic in the channel; however, walking the beach provides a more pleasant activity, with unobstructed views of Mt. Erie due north and Mt. Baker rising above Similk Bay to the northwest. The beach is passable during all but the highest tide; when high water forces the route inland, the bank can easily be climbed and the road walked for a distance. Hoypus Point, at road's end, is reached in slightly over a mile.

From 1912 until the Deception Pass bridge was completed in 1935, a ferry operated between here and Dewey Beach, linking Whidbey and Fidalgo Islands. A concrete bulkhead and piles, remnants of the old ferry landing can still be seen at the road end at Hoypus Point. Old newspaper accounts tell of the crowded ferry conditions on Sundays (even then!), when carloads of tourists would make springtime excursions to the park to picnic and to view the masses of pink wild rhododendrons.

Beyond the point the walking is even better, with a broader beach, views across the channel to Skagit, Kiket and Hope Islands. In about a mile, the park

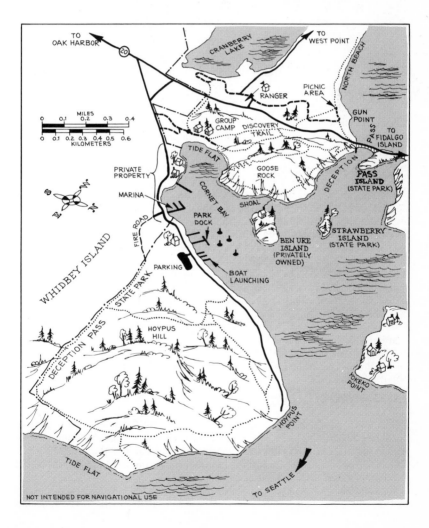

Clam digging

boundary is reached; the tide flat continues on for yet another mile to Ala Spit. Round trip from Cornet Bay to the park boundary and back is about 4 miles (6½ km).

STRAWBERRY ISLAND

Perhaps Strawberry is the perfect island; its 3 acres are just enough to assure visitors a measure of solitude in the middle of a busy freeway, while its shores are an insular rock garden bedecked with wind-shredded junipers and mossy granite slopes holding sedums and wild strawberries in their crannies. To this add the crowning touch—a stupendous view into the jaws of Deception Pass.

Salmon fishermen sometimes anchor just offshore, but the island itself is accessible only to canoes and other boats small enough to be drawn up on the rocky beaches. Skill and experience in boat handling are necessary to reach the island. Small boats should approach on a rising tide, when the flow will push the craft eastward into quieter water, rather than draw it into the pass, less than ½ mile away. Landing is easiest on the south and east sides, where the slopes flare more gently into the water.

Although the island is part of the state park, there are no camping amenities on shore. Please take any trash back home with you, and leave the island as pretty as when you arrived.

GOOSE ROCK AND GROUP CAMP

The state park's group camp, with rustic cabins, kitchen and dining hall (available for use by reservation), provides a base of operations for visiting environmental education groups. Camp facilities, located at the head of Cornet Bay, are reached via the turnoff road to the group camp, ½ mile (¾ km) east of the Highway 20/Cornet Bay Road intersection.

Low tide bares acres of eelgrass-coated mud flat in the bay, a marked contrast to the wave-scrubbed beaches on the west side of the park. While mucking about, examining the abundance of tiny marine life that inhabits the intertidal zone, be aware that the ½-mile section of property to the east, between the group camp and the state park dock is privately owned.

Towering nearly 500 feet above Cornet Bay, Goose Rock is a small echo of Mt. Erie to the north, with its glacier-scoured northern slope reflecting the south-bound course of an ancient icefield, and its near-vertical south face, to the lee of the glacier, exhibiting little evidence of such wearing.

Trails on the rock interweave, merge and sometimes end abruptly; at present very few are clearly signed. To hike its slopes, follow the service road past the group camp kitchen to the trailhead at the base of the hill. Shortly after entering the forest, the trail forks; the right hand branch is the Perimeter Trail, which circles the outer slopes around the rock, with views of Coronet Bay and Ben Ure Island before ducking into timber and eventually passing beneath the Deception Pass bridge and on to North Beach. The left hand trail branch goes clockwise to the northwest in a long, but gradual ascent to the summit of Goose Rock before looping back to a very steep, switchback descent to the Perimeter Trail.

A wide choice of side trails and alternate destinations make for an interesting variety of trips and scenery. Total distance for an average loop hike is about 3½ miles (5½ km); elevation gain via the "high road" is 475 feet (145 meters), via the "low road" about 200 feet (60 meters).

A less ambitious hike follows an abandoned road through a forest of sword fern and giant fir trees to North Beach. Find the trailhead for the North Beach Discovery Trail on the north side of the group camp behind the dining hall. The road was built during the time of CCC work in the park to give crews access to North Beach from Cornet Bay. The interesting rock and concrete underpass where the old road crosses beneath the highway was built at that time. Total distance to North Beach is ¾ mile (1 km), elevation gain 150 feet (450 meters).

DECEPTION PASS

One cannot fail to be impressed by the drama of Deception Pass, whether viewing it as a land-bound tourist from the heights of the 182-foot bridge, or experiencing it as a skipper attempting his first white-knuckle run through the narrow hallway. Measured against the timelessness of granite and the power of the boiling tidal current, man's great structural achievement of concrete and steel seems fragile indeed.

The entrance to the waterway was charted by early Spaniards, but it was the British sea captain George Vancouver who first explored it in 1792, and named it to express his feeling of deception, for he originally thought the pass was the mouth of the large bay indenting the peninsula which is now known to be Whidbey Island.

Before the days of engines, large sailing ships avoided the pass, unable to maneuver in its confines, instead choosing to sail southward along the outside shore of the island. Captain Thomas Coupe, who settled near Penn Cove in 1852, is said to be the only man to ever sail a fully rigged tall ship through the pass.

The rock-walled main channel of Deception Pass itself is scarcely 500 feet across, and Canoe Pass on the north is a claustrophobic 50 feet wide at its narrowest point, with a sharp bend along the way. It is, however, the current pouring through the channels and its associated churning eddys which are the concern of most skippers, for it reaches a velocity of up to eight knots as the granite spigot of the pass performs its twice-daily task of filling, then draining, then re-filling Skagit Bay.

Boat pilots are advised to consult local tidal current tables and run the pass during slack water, when the velocity of the current is at its minimum. Although fast boats do make the pass at other times, boat handling skill and knowledge of the local waters is advisable. High powered boats should stay well away from other boats in the channel, so their wake does not cause the less powerful vessels further distress.

The bridge, which was begun in 1934 and completed the following year, spans the gulf between Fidalgo and Whidbey Islands, utilizing little Pass Island for its central pillars. It required nearly 30 years of effort in state and national government to bring the bridge into being. As early as 1907 the link to Whidbey Island was urged in order to support the military garrison at Fort Casey and as an assistance to agricultural growth on Whidbey Island. Blueprints were prepared, but time and again hopes were dashed as funds for the project were failed to be appropriated.

Finally in 1933 the bridge appeared about to receive approval in the state legislature; Skagit and Island counties earmarked $150,000 in local funds and began work on the approaches to the span. However, once more the state legislature balked, and it was not until the following year, following some fast footwork by local politicians, that the money was finally approved (along with some matching funds from the federal Public Works Administration). In August the excavation of solid rock for the first pier of the bridge was begun.

A high-line with 4-ton capacity was rigged to Pass Island to transport the derrick for structural steel work, water lines were laid from Cranberry and Pass Lakes for mixing of the concrete and a month was spent building an aggregate bunker and cement warehouse. Month by month the steel fretwork grew against the sky, until slightly less than a year from the beginning of the first excavation,

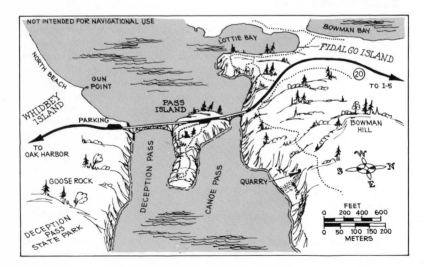

View east from Deception Pass bridge; Strawberry Island on left

the cantilevered spans stretching outward from Fidalgo Pass and Whidbey Islands were ready to be joined. Steelworkers clambering on the bridge under the hot sun of the July day were unable to align the two sections; however, in the cool of the following morning, when the metal had contracted enough to allow proper matching of the diagonals, the final joining was completed. Deception Pass was bridged.

PASS (CANOE) ISLAND

Parking areas at either end of the bridge and on Pass Island (which is sometimes known as Canoe Island) permit sightseers to leave their cars and walk along the span for a view of the pass which George Vancouver never had.

Trails eastward from the middle parking area traverse the rocky meadowland of grass, sedges, wildflowers and gnarled, weather-twisted trees on Pass Island. Use extreme care and keep a tight hand on small children, as the bluffs drop off steeply into the churning water. At the far eastern tip the slope gentles enough to enable hikers to reach the water's edge.

A magnificent display of underwater life on the walls of Goose Rock and around Pass Island rewards venturesome scuba divers, however the treacherous tidal current makes this an area only for the experts.

From the shore on the end of Pass Island, to the north in the cliff wall of Fidalgo Island, a gaping cave in the rock can be seen, and an outfall of talus below it. Some strange geological formation? No—remains of a rock quarry which was operated in conjunction with a state prison camp, through Walla Walla State Penitentiary, from 1909 until 1914.

A large wooden crusher was built below the quarry, stretching down the cliff to the water's edge. Rock dug from the quarry was put into the crusher, then mechanically sorted into bins and eventually loaded, via chutes, onto barges which were brought into Canoe Pass.

PRISON CAMP

For those with boats small enough to be landed on the beach, yet powerful enough to handle the tidal current so near to Canoe Pass, the site of the old penal colony can be explored. The small bay with its narrow beach is located due north of the eastern end of Pass Island.

Up to forty prisoners at a time lived in a stockade located on a flat just above the bay. Service buildings and homes of the prison guards were nearby. Only scant evidence of the colony remains—a round cistern, some bricks and scattered tiles, all nearly covered by brush.

Park rangers discourage hikers from climbing around in the cliffs in the vicinity of the quarry, as they are extremely dangerous. Be content to view it from the water or Pass Island.

CRANBERRY LAKE VICINITY

Access: Car
Facilities: Campsites (230 sites at Cranberry Lake), picnic tables, fireplaces, water, picnic shelters, kitchens, restrooms, bathhouse, showers, swimming beach, boat launch (on Cranberry Lake), playground
Attractions: Boating, canoeing, bicycling, fishing, hiking, beachcombing, swimming

Had that ancient glacier tried a little harder and dug a mere fifty feet deeper, Cornet Bay would have reached through to Rosario Strait, Goose Rock would have been an island and Cranberry Lake would never have come into being. As it was, a neck of land remained, joining Goose Rock to the glacial outfall of Whidbey Island; the Cranberry Lake area was merely a shallow, saltwater inlet of the sea.

Over the centuries wind and waves, sweeping in from the Strait of Juan de Fuca, built a sand bar which eventually joined to the rocks of West Point, forming a lagoon similar to those found in other places in the San Juans. However, instead of the brackish sea water entrapped in other lagoons, here an underground spring filled the shallow depression and changed the environment from salt to freshwater marsh, with cattails, willows, skunk cabbage, lily pads, muskrat, beaver, river otter and trout.

The Cranberry Lake entrance is on the west side of the road, slightly less than ¾ mile (1 km) south of the Deception Pass bridge on Highway 20. Near the entrance are the ranger's residence, service buildings and an information office. At the entrance to the park road, two intersections direct visitors first north, to the North Beach picnic area, then west to the campground and West Point, or south to the Cranberry Lake picnic area. At the second intersection is a large display board giving information on the park, and the trailhead for a ¼-mile self-interpreting nature walk.

This is one of the best bicycling areas in the park—with smooth and level roads, first wending through cool forest, then edging the lake shore. Tent sites for late-arriving bicyclists are guaranteed at Cranberry Lake Campground, even if the campground is filled with car campers.

The lake is only about 10 to 20 feet deep throughout, with its deepest point being a 40-foot "hole" near the north shore. It continues to be filled in with sediment; the closing-in of the lake margins is quite evident in photos taken over a period of years. In time, perhaps just a few hundred years, the lake will be completely filled in and overgrown with vegetation.

The lake, which is stocked with trout, is inviting for either fishing or quiet water paddling; boats with gasoline motors are not permitted. Muskeg bogs on the southwest bay can be reached only by water. Here the observant boater may spot beaver and muskrat lodges at the edge of the marsh.

CRANBERRY LAKE PICNIC AREA

This former campground on the east shore of Cranberry Lake is now reserved for day use only, with a spacious picnic area, tables and fireplaces shaded by giant timber, shelters with kitchens and a playground for small children.

Winter storm at West Point

A. FIDALGO ISLAND

A long T-shaped dock is a fine spot for fishermen to wet their lines; good swimming and wading in the enclosed space between dock and shore. Light-weight boats can be hand carried the distance from the parking lot to the water; those with heavier craft will prefer to launch them at the trailered boat ramp on the northwest bay of the lake.

A trail north from the picnic area leads along the shore to favorite fishing spots and lake viewpoints, joining the road to West Point in about ¼ mile.

CRANBERRY LAKE CAMPGROUND

The park's largest campground, kept open for year-around use, is located on the wooded arm between Cranberry Lake and North Beach. Follow signs west from the Cranberry Lake entrance on Highway 20 to the campground road. The upper (eastern) loop has 78 campsites, while the lower section, to the west, contains the remainder of the 230 sites. Both loops are sheltered by timber and have picnic tables, fireplaces, restrooms and showers.

WEST POINT AND WEST BEACH

Contained in this small area is probably the greatest diversity of environment within the park—forest, lake, cattail bogs, rocky headland, ocean surf and one of the finest sand beaches and dunelands on Puget Sound, all enhanced by views back to Mt. Erie and out across the Straits of Juan de Fuca to snowy Olympic peaks.

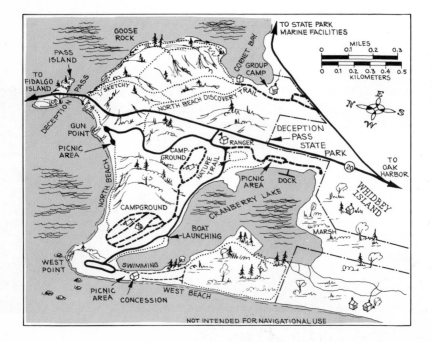

North Beach from Deception Pass bridge

A. FIDALGO ISLAND

On hot summer days, visitors may bathe at the supervised swimming area on the northwest beach of the bathwater-warm lake, or dash across the sand bar for a more invigorating dip in the frigid ocean. Picnic tables along the beach face on both the lake and the sound. Fires are permitted only in fireplaces. For lake exploration, boats may be launched on the ramp on the northwest shore.

Prospective beachcombers will find slim pickings on West Beach—waves sweeping in from the straits constantly shift the sand, making it an impossible environment for sea life. The beauty of the shore lies in its pristine, unbroken sweep, and in the dune area which backs it. A blacktop path leads into the dunes, now anchored by vegetation. Several picnic tables are along the path; a small wooden balcony provides an overview of the marsh.

In winter, when storm winds howl in from the ocean, sending waves crashing against the rocks at West Point, hardy souls who savor the excitement of marine pyrotechnics enjoy a visit to West Beach. Such storms are breathtaking—literally; at times they are so severe that it is impossible to stand against the force of the wind. Post-storm beachcombing often yields driftwood, agates, interesting flotsam and seafoam to play in.

Concrete footings at West Point are reminders of World War I times, when a searchlight was mounted here.

DECEPTION ISLAND

Lying less than ½ mile northwest of West Point, rugged Deception Island is the farthest outpost of the state park. Eastern approaches to the island are shallow and rock-riddled and the current can be strong; boaters should use great care. Immediately to the west the underwater shelf drops off quickly, making for excellent fishing and scuba diving just offshore.

Small boats may be beached on any of several rocky coves—the largest bay on the northwest side of the island is probably the easiest. Due to its difficult access and limited use, Deception Island has not been developed by the park and has no onshore amenities.

NORTH BEACH

Whether seen from the forest trail which traverses it, or from the water's edge, North Beach is one of the most popular areas in the park. The trailhead can be found on the outside loop of the lower campground or by heading east on any of several well-beaten paths from the West Point parking lot.

The nearly mile-long curve of the beach is broken by three rocky headlands. The most prominent of these, Gun Point, was the location of cannons which guarded the pass during World War I.

At low tide the beach is easily walked all the way from West Point to the base of the vertical cliffs below the bridge. Higher tides force the route inland at times for scrambles over the rocky bluffs or a retreat to the trail higher up in the trees. From the North Beach picnic area the trail continues east beneath the bridge and on to Goose Rock.

The swift current of the channel deters the growth of marine life on the gravel beach; however, agates are often turned up by the churning water. East of Gun Point hikers enjoy ant's-eye views of the bridge and, at slack tide, the parade of boats through the pass.

Sharpe Cove

NORTH BEACH PICNIC AREA

This day-use area in secluded timber and on the beach provides visitors with picnic tables, shelters, fireplaces and an always fascinating panorama of the pass.

To reach it, bear right immediately after driving through the park's Cranberry Lake entrance. The scenic route through the forest of huge old firs is worth the trip in itself. In just over ½ mile the parking lot is reached. Hiking trails along North Beach and around or over Goose Rock to Cornet Bay begin at the picnic area.

BOWMAN AND ROSARIO BAYS

Access: Car or boat
Facilities: Campsites (24 sites on Bowman Bay), picnic tables, fireplaces, water, picnic shelters, kitchens, restrooms, showers, boat launch, dock with float, fishing pier, playground
Attractions: Boating, fishing, scuba diving, hiking, tide pools

Yet another facet of this diverse park: here rounded bays facing away from the swirling current of the pass enable sea life to grow in profusion on rocks and beaches. Offshore, salmon runs attract fleets of commercial and sport fishermen.

A. FIDALGO ISLAND

Starfish

BOWMAN (RESERVATION) BAY

Nautical charts still designate this as Reservation Bay, a holdover from World War I when a military reservation was located there. Local residents, agreeing with the U.S. Geological Survey, prefer the name of Bowman Bay, in honor of the Fidalgo Island pioneer who had a summer cabin on its shore.

Bowman Bay is reached by car by following the signs at the intersection of Highway 20 at the west end of Pass Lake. The road which may be closed in winter, drops sharply downhill to a large open flat at the head of the bay.

The twenty-four-site campground is located in timber on the northern edge of the bay. Facilities include picnic tables, fireplaces, restrooms and a playground.

Bowman Bay offers some anchorages for boaters, although numerous rocks foul the entrance and care must be used on entering. The bay is open to swells from Rosario Strait, and an overnight stay may be uncomfortable.

Although much smaller than Bowman Bay, Sharpe Cove to the north, tucked behind Rosario Head, is usually a better spot for a layover. The park maintains a small dock with float on the cove, and there is space for several other good anchorages.

Until recently the Department of Fisheries operated a fish hatchery on Bowman Bay; however, the facility is now closed. A long stationary pier on the bay is a remnant of the defunct hatchery. While it is a fine place from which to fish, it is largely unusable by pleasure boaters, for tying to the widely spaced, vertical pilings is difficult and the dock level is so high above the water that disembarking is impossible except at the ladder on the north side.

The gravel ramp between the pier and the campground is the only launching area for trailered boats in this section of the park.

RESERVATION HEAD

The path south along the shore of Bowman Bay leads to hiking trails which traverse Reservation Head and a smaller, unnamed headland lying east of Lottie Bay. Climbing high on exposed, grassy bluffs, the trails offer views into Deception Pass, across to Cranberry Lake and out to the inviting blue-green islands of the San Juans.

Shallow Lottie Bay separates the two cliffy headlands. Long ago Bowman and Lottie Bays were joined as a continuous waterway; over the years wave action built the sand neck which creates the two bays, linking Reservation Head to Fidalgo Island.

At extremely low tide Lottie Bay is nearly drained. Its muddy bottom is home for many kinds of interesting sea life. The shoreline can be followed past tiny, rock-walled coves clear around to the neck connecting Lighthouse Point, where a trail can be followed back to Bowman Bay. Use care not to become trapped on the rocks by the incoming tide.

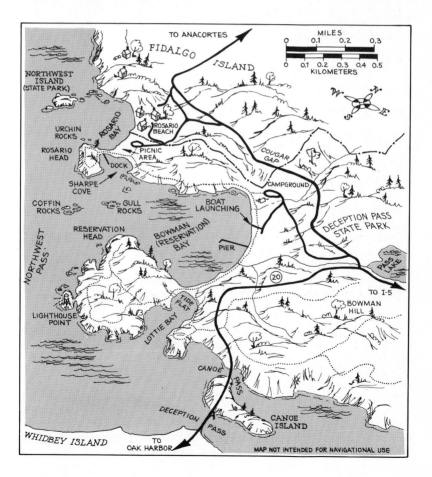

Scuba divers at Rosario Bay; Northwest Island on right

An average loop stroll from the Bowman Bay parking lot, around either headland and back again is about 2 miles (3¼ km); elevation gain 150 feet (50 meters).

ROSARIO BAY

The state park shares this choice bay with a university marine research facility and a number of private homes. To reach the beach, at Pass Lake turn north from Highway 20 onto the Rosario road (Highway 525). In about a mile (1½ km), signs direct motorists to Rosario Beach. Follow the road to the state park property, avoiding private side roads.

The spacious picnic area with tables and fireplaces faces on Rosario Bay and Sharpe Cove. Rustic shelters with kitchens accommodate large gatherings; modern restrooms have outside showers for rinsing saltwater from bodies and scuba gear.

The bay is legendary among divers and marine biologists for its extravaganza of sea life. It is a rococo world of flamboyant anemone, sea pens, nudibranches, sponges and one of the largest concentrations of purple and green sea urchins to be found on the inland waters. The rocks lying just off Rosario Head are well named as Urchin Rocks.

The bay itself is suitable for snorkelers and for divers with beginning skill; greater experience is needed to venture out of the bay into deeper, swifter water. At low tide rocks form tide pools and give land-bound sightseers a glimpse of what lies beneath the water. Remember that this is a marine preserve and the taking or destruction of any marine life is prohibited.

NORTHWEST ISLAND

Northwest Island, ½ mile northwest of the Rosario Beach picnic area is yet another of the park's small undeveloped islands. The grassy, 1-acre rock is visited mainly by sea gulls and scuba divers. Although it lies temptingly close, divers are advised to take a boat to the island rather than to attempt to swim the distance, for the tidal current is very strong.

ROSARIO TRAILS

A ¼-mile loop trail beginning at the picnic area invites visitors upwards to the modest heights of Rosario Head. Barren slopes on the outer brow of the hill offer miles-wide panoramas of the San Juan Islands, the straits and the bustling boat traffic.

Eastward from the picnic ground a bluff-top trail circles Sharpe Cove and Bowman Bay, dropping down to the campground in about a mile. Lanky firs along the trail extend horizontally out over the water, supported by but a few roots. Possibly the next storm will see their demise, or perhaps they will still be stubbornly clinging there when your grandchildren hike the trail.

PASS LAKE AREA

Access: Car
Facilities: Boat launch
Attractions: Boating, fishing, hiking

PASS LAKE

Water holds its own special fascination, whether ocean swells surging through narrow, rocky channels, placid waves lapping on sandy beaches, or brackish marshes choked with cattails and frogs. Here the state park offers 100 acres of crystal clear water for trout fishing or still water canoeing.

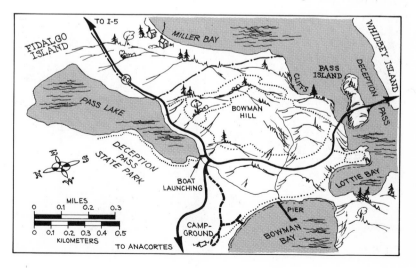

A. FIDALGO ISLAND

Originally the park only owned land bordering on the western end of the lake; however, the remainder of the surrounding lands were recently acquired, including property reaching clear to Lake Campbell. The forested areas are presently undeveloped. A sketchy trail, established by the boots of determined fishermen, follows the north shore of the lake.

Pass Lake lies at the junction of Highway 20 and the Rosario Road (Highway 525). A gravel public boat ramp and parking lot adjoin the intersection. Some pull-offs where the road parallels the lakeshore provide more parking, spots to put in lightweight boats and waterfront picnic sites.

The trout-stocked lake is open to fly-fishing only during regular fishing season; gasoline motors are not permitted. Canoeists will find idyllic paddling the length of the lake and along its brushy shoreline.

Deer, muskrat, skunk, fox and other small wild animals may be seen on shore, especially at dusk. In winter migratory ducks stop to rest on the lake, floating together in convivial rafts.

BOWMAN HILL

Visitors to Deception Pass State Park usually seek out the beaches and water-oriented viewpoints, for they are its unique features. The demand has not been great for woodland trails, although there is ample space for a fine system of such paths at Bowman Hill, Hoypus Hill and Pass Lake.

Bowman Hill, at 528 feet the highest point in the park, has the potential of providing secluded forest walks coupled with stunning panoramas from bald viewpoints. At present over 2 miles of unimproved trails, following power lines and old military service roads, loop around and over the top of the hill. Recommended only for hikers experienced in route finding, the trails begin at the pullout just north of the bridge on Fidalgo Island. The south slope of the hill is extremely cliffy; hikers are warned to stay well away from the edge.

Cinnamon teal

B. BELLINGHAM CHANNEL

Situated north of Anacortes, two large islands and their entourage of smaller islets have managed to escape both creeping real estate development and industrialization. Although separated only by mile-wide Bellingham Channel, neighboring Cypress and Guemes Islands are totally different in character. While Guemes has a rural atmosphere, with wide expanses of flatland and a long, smooth shoreline, Cypress Island is steep, rocky and densely wooded, with deeply-notched bays and a cliffy shoreline.

Smaller Sinclair and Vendovi Islands, to the north, in the front door to Bellingham Bay, are privately owned and have little to attract tourists, although their bays and shoreline offer interesting boat exploration. A long shoal extends out from Sinclair Island on the north and east, reaching almost to Boulder Reef—use care at low tide.

Cone Islands, a cluster of miniature forested islands and low-tide rocks, lying off the northeast shore of Cypress Island, are undeveloped state park lands. With steep, rocky shores and surrounding kelp beds, most boaters are content to enjoy the islands from the distance as they cruise by; although scuba divers do sometimes stop there for underwater exploration.

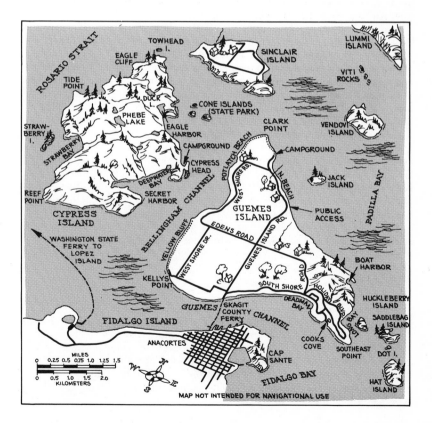

B. BELLINGHAM CHANNEL

GUEMES ISLAND

Access: Ferry or boat
**Facilities (at resort and county park): Groceries, fuel, cabins, boat launching,
    boat rental, campsites, picnic tables, water, fireplaces, restrooms, showers**
Attractions: Boating, fishing, beachcombing, clams, bicycling

Guemes Island would be just another Anacortes suburb were it not for the
½-mile water barrier of Guemes Channel which serves to keep urban sprawl and
industrial boom at arm's length. At one time the island was eyed as a prospective
site for an aluminum processing plant, however the adverse reaction of residents
sent developers looking elsewhere.

The island remains quietly pastoral, providing sanctuary for retirees, artists,
farmers, summer vacationers and Fidalgo Island workers who commute daily
from their homes.

The little ferry *Almar* scurries back and forth across the channel like a busy
waterbug, carrying a few cars on its open deck each trip. The voyage takes about
10 minutes; runs are made hourly through the day. The ferry, which is operated
by Skagit County, not by the state, leaves from a terminal in downtown
Anacortes at 6th and I Streets.

Guemes is ideal bicycling country, with straight and level interior roads that
bypass farmlands and orchards, while perimeter roads wind around the shores,
with views out to cool sea and distant islands.

The only "commercial" development on Guemes is a small resort on the
northern tip of the island, which has a few cabins, a campground, boats for rent
and launching facilities. The adjacent county park, which is also managed by the
resort, has additional campsites in an open meadow above the shore. Although
the resort has boat facilities, it has no dock. Since it is located on a shallow tide
flat, even small boats should approach with care.

Guemes has a refreshing approach to public use of lands: here numerous
beaches and some forested areas are posted as "Open Space" (a sharp contrast to
the "No Trespassing" signs so prevalent in San Juan County). Owners of such
lands permit public recreational use, as long as such use is compatible with its
natural state; in other words, observe posted fire regulations, do not litter and do
not deface or destroy either property or natural features.

The areas described below are presently posted as open space. If their status
changes, do not trespass—look elsewhere for recreational land.

KELLYS POINT

A spur road continues west from the intersection of South Shore Drive and
West Shore Drive to a beautiful gravel and driftwood beach facing Bellingham
Channel. The beach can be walked north for more than a mile, beneath the
imposing 150-foot scarp of Yellow Bluff. Climbing on the bluff, or digging caves
can be hazardous, as the bank is composed of soft glacial till and can collapse.
Note the numerous holes that birds have burrowed in the hillside.

The point is named after the notorious outlaw, Lawrence "Smuggler" Kelly,
who had a hideout here in the 1870s.

Top left: raccoons; bottom left: river otters; right: raccoon tracks on beach

CLARK POINT

Nearly 2 miles (3 km) of beautiful, clean gravel beach wrap around the point, providing terrific views first into Bellingham Bay, then north to Sinclair, Vendovi and Lummi Islands, then finally swinging westward to lovely little Cone Islands and mountainous Cypress.

To reach the beach, drive to the northern end of the Guemes Island Road and walk north from the resort. Near the point the beach narrows, but should be passable at all but the highest tide or during heavy wave action. The bank above the beach is steep and heavily wooded, and there is no inland egress, so use care not to get trapped by high water. Open space ends at private property on Potlatch Beach on the eastern side of the point.

NORTH BEACH

Facing on a huge tide flat is a densely settled area of beach-front homes and summer cottages, reminiscent of Hood Canal. A narrow public access to the beach is provided for clam diggers. Watch carefully amid the cottages for a small sign on the east side of the road, near the south end of the beach. Hand carried boats can be launched here.

Cooks Cove lagoon

BOAT HARBOR (SQUARE HARBOR)

The hilly, eastern tip has the only forest hike on the island. To find the trailhead, follow South Shore Road east from the ferry landing to a three-way intersection in about 1½ miles (2½ km). Go straight ahead on Holiday Boulevard, and in slightly over ½ mile (¾ km), turn left onto a broad, dirt road. Soon a wide spot with parking space for several cars is reached. Park and walk, for from here on the road deteriorates badly.

The path descends through cool, second-growth timber where, in fall, nearly a dozen different types of mushrooms can be found. In ½ mile (¾ km) the tiny square-shaped harbor is reached. There are several primitive campsites in the trees above the bay.

Facing southeasterly, the bay offers protected anchorages for two or three boats—a handy spot when nearby Saddlebag Island is filled to overflowing.

COOKS COVE

A public boat launch ramp is located on the eastern tip of the island, facing on Guemes Channel. To reach it, follow South Shore Road east from the ferry landing to the first intersection. Here turn right onto Channel View Drive, and continue to bear right to the road end at Cooks Cove.

The small cove, backed by a pretty little lagoon looks out to the imposing headland of Cap Sante and the oil refineries of March Point.

CYPRESS ISLAND

For the past several years Cypress Island has been dangled temptingly before the noses of recreationists and conservationists as a site for a future state park and natural preserve. In 1978 hopes of the state purchasing a large portion of the island were dashed when 2,500 acres of available land were sold, not to the Department of Natural Resources, but to a private interest.

As of 1979, about 800 acres of the 5,500-acre island, and about half the tidelands are state owned. Unfortunately, the upland property is at four different locations in the interior, making it largely inaccessible. It is possible that in the future more lands will be acquired by the state, and shore access will permit some public use.

Cypress Island, the most nearly virginal of all the San Juans, can be reached only by boat. Although there has been some mining, and the forests have been selectively logged, the steep terrain and difficulty of access have discouraged real estate development. Its natural riches include six spring-fed lakes, several marshes, three excellent harbors, magnificent fortress-like cliffs, and forested mountains reaching to 1,500 feet.

More than eighty species of birds and a dozen kinds of mammals live here, including bald eagles, deer, fox, river otter, raccoon, porcupine, muskrat and weasels. The unusual geological strata supports a great variety of flora, however one notable tree is missing, for Captain George Vancouver erroneously named the island when he identified the local juniper trees as cypress—there are no cypress on Cypress Island.

B.   BELLINGHAM CHANNEL

Several different private groups, including The Nature Conservancy, have been involved in efforts to "save Cypress Island". Unfortunately disagreement between these groups in the acceptable balance between public recreation and natural preservation has kept them from working together effectively, while state agencies, hobbled by lack of funds and the slow-turning wheels of government have missed opportunities to pick up available lands.

There is no question that this splendid island should be saved from the chain saw and bulldozer and preserved in a natural state for present and future generations. In addition to state funds, some federal monies may be made available for the project. Active public support of the efforts of the Department of Natural Resources to obtain property here, or support of any other agency or private group involved in preserving the island, may well provide the impetus to yet save Cypress Island.

Cypress Island forest

Ferry travelers have an excellent view of Cypress Island as the boat leaves the Anacortes terminal, for its southern tip lies just 2½ nautical miles across Guemes Channel to the north. Its northwest shore is a popular salmon fishing grounds, and cruising boaters sometimes drop anchor in Deepwater Bay and Eagle Harbor along the eastern shore. Strawberry Bay, on the west, is less protected, but does offer good anchorages in calm weather.

Strawberry Bay was visited in 1792 by William Broughton, a lieutenant of Vancouver's expedition, who first explored the inner channels of the San Juan Islands. Broughton anchored here in his brig *Chatham* and was delighted to find great numbers of wild strawberries on shore. Some days later when Vancouver stopped over in the same spot, at Broughton's recommendation, the strawberries were out of season, and his crew had to settle for wild onions. (Be grateful it's not named Onion Bay.)

STRAWBERRY (LOON) ISLAND

Park Area: 11 acres
Access: Boat only
Facilities: Picnic tables, fireplaces, no water, pit toilet

A ¼-mile long, narrow ridge of an island just off Strawberry Bay is the site of a DNR campground. Strawberry Island, like several of the other small park islands, is composed of two high, rounded shoulders of land joined by a low, narrow neck—in this case the northern shoulder is considerably larger and higher than the southern one.

The shores of the main section of the island are so steep that going ashore there is quite difficult. The only landing for small boats is at a sandy cove on the southeast side of the neck. Offshore waters are quite deep and have defied attempts to place buoys. Large boats should anchor in Strawberry Bay and dinghy across to the island.

The island offers a few picnic and campsites, along with pleasant shoreline scrambles and views of boats parading by in Rosario Strait.

CYPRESS HEAD

Park Area: 12 acres
Access: Boat only
Facilities (by summer of 1980): Mooring buoys, dock with float, campsites, fireplaces, pit toilets, no water

On the eastern-most bulge of Cypress, joined to the parent island by a narrow sandspit, is a low, wooded "tombolo" known as Cypress Head. The head, spit and several acres on Cypress Island are being developed by the DNR as a fine boat-in campground with moorage and camping accommodations for several boats.

This pretty little spot is only 4 nautical miles from the boat launching ramp at Sunset Beach on Fidalgo Island, making it an ideal cruising destination. The long, south-facing bay formed by the head is quite shallow and has a rock near the entrance; use care entering. The dock and mooring buoys will be in the deeper, northern cove.

Willow Island from ferry

C. THATCHER PASS

The "front door" to the San Juan heartland, Thatcher Pass is the thoroughfare for much of the island's pleasure boating and all of its ferry traffic. Although the ½-mile wide channel has ample room for all the vessels which pass through it, it may seem snug quarters for sailboats trying to make way in light wind when a monstrous green and white ferry is hard astern.

Thatcher Pass provides westbound ferry passengers with their first "arm's reach" views as the boat threads its way between Decatur and Blakely Islands. Tourists "ooh and aah" at little Armitage Island and its twin bays, and perhaps with a start they notice that there is a stately bald eagle perched atop a pine snag surveying them.

Ferry boat captains, possibly bored with the routine, have been known to whip the wheel hard to starboard here and cut between Blakely and Willow Island to give passengers a heart-stopping closer look.

BLAKELY AND DECATUR ISLANDS

Facilities (at Peavine Pass on Blakely Island): transient moorage, dock, fuel, groceries, laundry, showers

Like two guardians poised at either side of Thatcher Pass, Blakely and Decatur Islands stand as protectors of the inner channels of the San Juans, their eastern shores bearing the brunt of storms whipping down Rosario Strait.

68

Blakely Island, the largest, highest and most imposing of the pair lies to the north of the pass. At the far northern end of the island, facing on Peavine Pass, is a marina—its only tourist facility. Fuel and temporary moorage are available at the float in the outer harbor, overnight moorage slips are in the inner harbor; the entrance is shallow, but well-marked. The island airport is immediately to the southwest. Don't plan on shore leave here, for all island roads are private and are gated just beyond the marina.

Several nice anchorages can be found around the island behind pretty little Armitage Island on the south, and in Thatcher Bay. Beware of submerged pilings on the north side of the bay.

Most of Blakely Island is owned by a small corporation which purchased the land from a logging company. It sells only a few home sites each year in order to insure the island's orderly development. Such exclusiveness stems not from snobbery or for a desire for inflated real estate prices, but from a great love for this delicate island and concern for the welfare of the people who build their homes there. Boaters should respect their intent and admire the island from the water, but stay off private property.

Seattle Pacific University has been deeded several sections of the island, including beach lands and property bordering on the two lakes, for a total of 960 acres—more than 1/5th of the total island acreage. The property was donated to the University to be used in its natural state for research and educational programs.

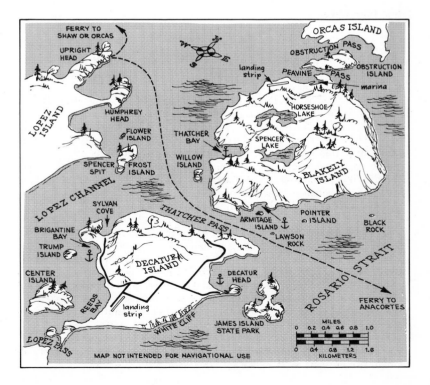

Great blue heron

Black Rock, Pointer Island and Lawson Rock, lying east of Blakely, along Rosario Strait, along with Willow Island on the west side, are all part of the San Juan Islands Wilderness.

Just half the size of its neighbor to the north, and with less-dramatic contours, Decatur may not seem as exclusive as Blakely, but its lands also are all private. A short dock is located on the southwest end of the island on Reads Bay at Decatur (the few houses there can't really be called a town). Nearby is the island airplane landing strip; there are no stores or boating facilities on shore.

Some good anchorages can be found at Brigantine Bay, a bit to the north behind Trump Island. Shrimp pots set here usually bring in enough of the tasty crustaceans to enhance a galley dinner.

Around a rocky headland is another fine anchorage in Sylvan Cove, known locally as Kan Kut Bay. The neat farm buildings and velvet pastures of San Elmo at the head of the bay are an idyllic scene from the water. All property surrounding the cove, including the dock, is posted.

On the east shore of Decatur is a large, curving bight with gentle, sandy beach, punctuated by the round knob of Decatur Head. The head, known geologically as a tombolo, was once a separate little island, but the action of wind and waves over centuries of time, built up the sand neck which now joins it to the larger island. Spencer Spit, just to the west on Lopez Island, is an example of such a neck in the process of being formed.

The south end of the bight, behind the protection of Decatur Head, offers some good anchorages to overflow crowds from James Island State Park, although care must be used anchoring here, as it is quite shallow.

JAMES ISLAND STATE PARK

Park Area: 113 acres
Access: Boat only
Facilities: Campsites, picnic tables, pit toilets, dock with float, mooring buoys,
   no water
Attractions: Clamming, swimming, fishing, hiking, scuba diving

Lacking the broad beaches and sheltered harbors of other San Juan marine parks, James Island is often ignored by visitors in favor of more glamorous spots. Its coves are frequently used only as an overnight stop for southbound boaters awaiting the turn of the tide at Deception Pass. Nevertheless the park offers pleasant camping and scenic hikes to those who linger awhile.

One of the more rugged of the San Juan Island State Parks, its high, steep bluffs are broken by two small coves on opposing sides of the island. The cove on the west, protected from weather by Decatur Island, contains a dock with float large enough for three or four boats and a single mooring buoy. Decatur Head lies immediately west across the ½-mile channel, tethered to its parent island by a narrow spit of land. The eastern cove, with four mooring buoys, is broader and open to weather and waves from Rosario Strait.

James is 4 nautical miles west of Sunset Beach or Flounder Bay on Fidalgo Island, the nearest point where trailered boats can be launched. Small, hand carried boats can be launched at Spencer Spit on Lopez Island which is 4 nautical miles to the west. Tidal currents can reach 7 knots in Thatcher Pass, so passage from Lopez Island to James in a very small or unpowered boat can be hazardous. Heavy weekend traffic in the channel adds to the danger.

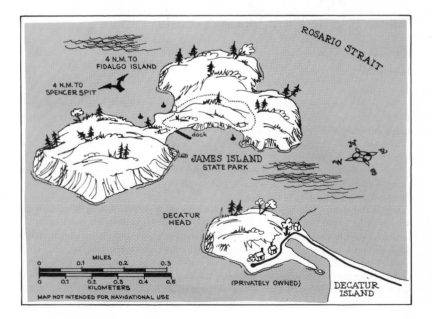

James Island forest

The deep water of the coves and strong current, especially on the west side, make anchoring difficult if the buoys and float are occupied, but small boats may easily be beached at either cove.

The western cove is a favorite scuba diving area; while fish are few, the invertebrate life is varied and colorful.

Scattered in the trees on the neck of land between the two coves, a dozen campsites provide picnic tables, fireplaces and pit toilets, but no fresh water; campers must furnish their own.

From the camp area a broad, signed trail meanders into deep forest, arriving in ½ mile at a tiny beach on the far edge of the western cove with two campsites in the forest above the beach. A secluded driftwood-strewn beach on the south flank of the island may be reached by boat or overland exploration.

Many ill-defined paths lace the island, some of them marked with colored plastic streamers. Use care in following these paths along the high grassy bluffs as many of them dwindle away. Overzealous exploration can leave a hiker hung up on the cliffs, or an unwary step can result in a bad fall into the rocks or water.

Clam digging at Spencer Spit

D. LOPEZ ISLAND

Cow country—and sheep and goats and horses, too. A green patchwork quilt of fields and pastures, interrupted by sections of velvety forest, rolling down to the edge of the sea. Farmyards with chickens busily scratching around great piles of fishing nets. Arrow-straight roads, edged by fences, disappearing into soupy San Juan mists. Only at its southern tip does the level land tilt upward to form steep, craggy cliffs and deeply notched, rocky bays. As if to compensate for its meek, pastoral nature, here Lopez presents come of the most rugged shoreline to be found in any of the San Juans.

Lopez Island does not display as much of the distinct marine flavor that Orcas and San Juan Islands exude. Its shoreline does not attract the hordes of yachtsmen, for it lacks the good harbors necessary to such activities. Bays on the north are quite shallow, while those on the south are farther from the boating mainstream, and are subject to bad weather and uncomfortable swells from the Strait of Juan de Fuca. Nevertheless, several choice spots along its shore do make fine stopovers for boat-bound tourists, and the gently rolling heartland is a joy to hikers and bicyclists.

D. LOPEZ ISLAND

The island is reached by ferry from Anacortes (about a 45-minute trip), or from Sidney, B.C. on Vancouver Island (slightly less than 2 hours away). The ferry landing is in a cove at the tip of Upright Head, where the only tourist facility is a small coffee shop. City folk, visiting the San Juans for the first time, have been known to unload their cars at Lopez, drive down the timber-bordered road of Upright Head, make a quick loop around the island, and scurry back to the next departing ferry, shocked at the lack of civilized amenities.

Lopez Island may be reached by San Juan Airlines, which stops at the local airfield, by prior reservation. A charter service based at the Lopez airport also makes flights throughout the San Juans and western Washington.

At the entrance to Fisherman Bay, on the west side of the island, is the village of Lopez, where a post office, grocery store, gas station, and a few shops do business; this is the island "shopping center". A marina with restaurant and motel ¾ mile (1 km) south of Lopez on Fisherman Bay, has overnight accommo-

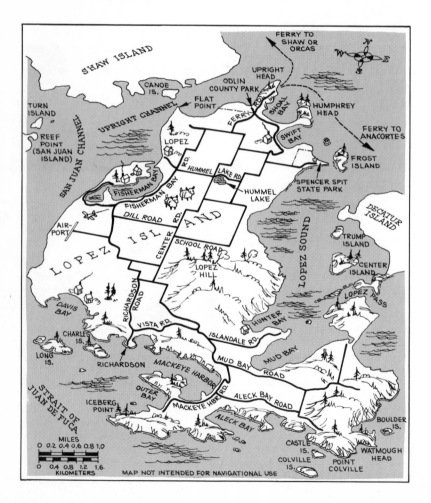

dations. Meals are also offered at an inn located on the south end of the island at Mackaye Harbor. The small general store at Richardson has groceries, fuel and marine supplies.

Odlin County Park and Spencer Spit State Park, two public campgrounds with a total of forty-five sites, provide the only available camping on Lopez Island—not a great deal during the busy summer season. Camping along the road is prohibited; check into a campground early in the day, and if unable to find a site, go elsewhere.

Obviously such limited accommodations (both camping and motels) can become overloaded in summer. Better to visit the island off season—it is no less lovely, and far less hectic.

THE NORTH END

ODLIN COUNTY PARK

Park Area: 80 acres
Access: Ferry to Lopez Island, boat
Facilities: Campsites, picnic tables, picnic shelters, group camp, fireplaces, water, pit toilets, boat launching ramp, dock with float, playground
Attractions: Beachcombing, fishing, boating, swimming, clams

Truly a family park, with a beached rowboat where youngsters can play at "going to sea" with driftwood oars, an old cannon to climb on, and an open field for family ballgames or Frisbee matches. All this and an outstanding beach, too.

Odlin Park

D. LOPEZ ISLAND

Odlin Park

Odlin Park is located within minutes of the ferry terminal at Upright Head. To reach it, follow Ferry Road south from the ferry landing for 1¼ mile (2 km); at a two-way intersection turn right (west), and follow the road downhill for 300 yards (275 meters) to the campground on a curving, sandy bay. The park makes a nice quick stop for lazing in the sun while waiting for the next ferry—and perhaps to decide to linger awhile and catch a later one.

A trailered boat launch is straight ahead at the road end; a branch to the left leads past the ballfield to the campground. Beneath sheltering trees are some thirty sites, including a few walk-in camps located along the bank overlooking the bay. The road continues on to a clearing with a large campsite designed for group get-togethers.

By boat, the park lies 3½ nautical miles southeast of Orcas, and 5½ nautical miles east northeast of Friday Harbor. A dock with a float on the north end of the park will hold a few boats. Larger ones will prefer to anchor out as the bay is quite shallow.

The fine sandy beach invites swimming, sand castle building and barefoot walks. At low tide clams may be dug—if those ahead of you haven't got them already. Just offshore the ferry sails by in Upright Channel on the "direct to Friday Harbor" run which omits stops at Shaw and Orcas Islands. The beach can be walked from one end of the park to the other, a distance of nearly a mile, until uprising cliffs halt progress.

Trails out of the campground circle around in a flatland of second-growth timber and brush. Some deadend, others loop back to meet the campground road. Good mushroom picking in season. A shore-side trail goes past two walk-in campsites and up the gradually steepening embankment, 100 feet above the water. Use care as the edge is undercut and can be dangerous—not recommended for children.

Land south of the campground at Flat Point, known as Bella Tierra, is owned by the Department of Natural Resources. In the past it was considered for development as an additional camp area and recreational site, but the idea received negative reaction from surrounding property owners.

If recreationists can convince the DNR of their desire for the campground, and residents of the benefits to be gained from such a development, it may be possible that the area will be opened for public recreation. Letters regarding this property or any other DNR lands in the San Juans should be sent to: Commissioner of Public Lands, Department of Natural Resources, Public Lands Bldg., Olympia, Washington 98504.

FISHERMAN BAY AND LOPEZ

Access: Ferry to Lopez Island, boat
Facilities: Transient moorage with electric hookups and water, boat launching, boat rental, marine repair, fuel, restrooms, showers, picnic area, groceries, stores, restaurant, motel
Attractions: Boating, canoeing, bicycling, fishing, crabs, clams

Fisherman Bay could more aptly be named Fisherman Lagoon, for with its shallow bottom, stagnant water and mud-flat barrier built up by wave action, it is more closely related to the small lagoons found throughout the San Juans than the clear, deep-water bays. But such a lagoon! Nearly ½ mile across and more than 1 mile in length, with shimmering, tranquil waters and evening sunsets to bring tears to the eyes.

Many boatmen bypass Fisherman Bay, feigning disinterest, but instead are apprehensive about the shallow entrance channel. Once this barrier is conquered, however, any yachtsman can lean back with the air of an experienced

Congregational Church, built in 1904, near village of Lopez

D. LOPEZ ISLAND

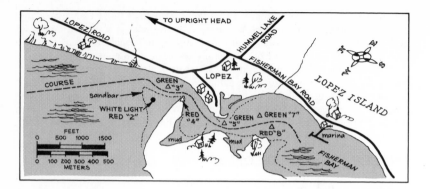

salt and play one-upmanship with less accomplished skippers. It is claimed by businesses inside the bay that any boat that does not draw more than 4½ feet (that's 1.37 meters for Canadians), can enter the bay safely if the tide is not below zero. If that statement does not totally reassure a skipper, enter on a rising tide to avoid the embarrassment of being stuck on a sand bar through a change of tide.

The accompanying map should be helpful when navigating the channel. Once into the channel keep red, even numbered markers to starboard, green odd numbered to port when entering, the opposite when returning.

If the anxious moments of the channel can be forgotten, the ½-mile journey is delightful, especially to large boats unaccustomed to such close quarters— cruising through the front yard of quaint little waterfront homes, with the banks almost within arm's reach.

Moorage, fuel and supplies are available at the marina on the east shore, or treat yourself to dinner at the restaurant. Good anchorages can be had farther into the bay.

To reach Lopez and Fisherman Bay from the ferry landing, follow Ferry Road south for 2¼ miles (3½ km). At a T intersection turn right (west), and in ½ mile (¾ km) turn left (south) onto Fisherman Bay Road. In 2 miles (3 km) the road to Lopez is on the right; turn here or continue on to Fisherman Bay, 5½ miles (8¾ km) total distance from Upright Head.

The village of Lopez, at the entrance to the bay has several stores, but no dock. The motel, restaurant, marina and marine center are ¾ mile (1 km) down the road to the south.

The bay is superb for small boat paddling. Put in hand carried boats at Lopez or at the marina and explore the channel and around the bay. Drop off a crab pot near the western shore and return in the morning to find it filled with Dungeness—perhaps.

A startling sight from the road at Fisherman Bay, especially at high tide, are cars virtually driving on water across the low sand spit at the head of the bay to reach a forested peninsula. This narrow neck of land is interesting to drive or bike, but spectacular to walk. To reach it, turn west at the south end of the bay and follow the road as it curves around the mudflat. There is parking space midway along the spit or at its northern end. Abandon cars and walk along the narrow spit, either on the beach or at road's edge.

Within a few feet of one another are two entirely different saltwater environments. Inside the bay is grassy, saltwater marsh, where crabs, clams, tiny fish

Marsh hawk

and myriad other small critters live, and where sea birds gather to feed and rest. Outside is smooth, clean beach with wave-swept sand and silvered driftwood, but relatively little shore life. The constant movement of waves from San Juan Channel prevents the growth of marine life here.

HUMMEL LAKE

Area: 36 acres
Facilities: Boat launching ramp
Attractions: Fishing, bird watching, canoeing

Here's a modest little pond, only 10 feet deep and 500 yards across, but a favorite with trout fishermen, a pleasant spot for wildlife-watchers and big enough for canoeists to take a brief paddle. The lake is located on the Hummel Lake Road, ¾ mile (1 km) due east of the village of Lopez.

To reach it from the ferry landing, follow Ferry Road south for 2¼ miles (3½ km) to a T intersection. Turn left (east), then in ¼ mile (⅓ km) right onto Center Road which can be followed to the lake, about 4½ miles (7¼ km) total distance from the start.

The public boat launch and parking area is on Center Road, just south of the Hummel Lake Road intersection. A bronze plaque at the edge of the parking lot tells that the lake is named in honor of pioneer Elwin Harry Hummel, who settled on the island in 1876.

It's a quiet place, since boats with gasoline motors are not permitted, and the cattails and blackberries which edge the lake rustle with bird life. In addition to the usual assortment of ducks and marsh birds which frequent such ponds, look for marsh hawks who hunt the area, searching for small rabbits and birds.

The lake is stocked regularly with rainbow trout.

SPENCER SPIT STATE PARK

Park Area: 129 acres
Access: Ferry to Lopez Island or boat
Facilities: Campsites, picnic tables, stoves, beach fire rings, water, pit toilets, mooring buoys
Attractions: Clams, crabs, shrimp, fishing, bicycling, beachcombing, swimming, canoeing

The popularity of Spencer Spit State Park on Lopez Island grows with each new "discovery" by camper, bicyclists and boaters. Visitors delight in the many activities which the beaches and waters offer and in the marine view. To the north, tiny Flower Island nestles against the imposing backdrop of Orcas Island. At sunset the channel is bathed in afterglow as the lights of ferries glimmer against Orcas' dark silhouette.

To reach the park from the ferry landing at Upright Head, drive 1¼ miles (2 km) to the first road junction and turn left on Port Stanley Road. At 3¾ miles (6 km) turn left onto Baker View Road, continuing straight ahead to the park in 5 miles (8 km). The park is 4½ nautical miles by boat southwest of Obstruction Pass on Orcas Island, where boats can be launched.

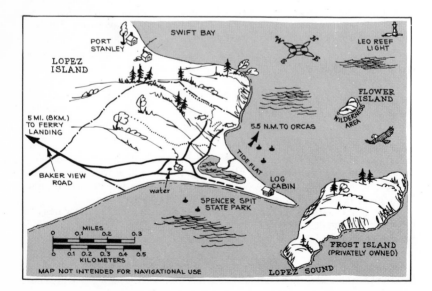

View from Spencer Spit State Park; Flower Island on left, Blakely Island on right

In summer the sixteen campsites strung along the beach are usually crowded with trailers and pickup campers. A spur road higher on the hill leads to primitive campsites for bicyclists and backpackers (no car parking space); farther along the spur road is an area for group camping. Picnic tables with stoves and fire rings located on the beach invite daytime picnicking and evening bonfires; build fires only in designated areas.

A dozen mooring buoys scattered on either side of the spit accommodate boaters, with plenty of space for additional boats to drop anchor. There is no trailered boat launching area at the park, however small boats can easily be hand carried the short distance from the car to the beach.

Winter storms toss up driftwood and shells for beachcombers on the mile-long sandy beach. Butter, horse and littleneck clams can be dug during summer low tides, and the waters yield crab, shrimp and bottomfish. During warm summer days the broad beaches heat the usually frigid water to bearable swimming temperatures.

Spencer Spit is an excellent example of a sandspit enclosing a saltchuck lagoon commonly found in the San Juans. These lagoons are formed over a long period of time by the action of wind and tide on sandy beaches. In many cases lagoons of this type eventually fill with sediment and no longer contain water.

A wide variety of birds pause at the lagoon during migration, including several kinds of gulls, a dozen types of ducks, great blue herons, kingfishers, black brandt and Canadian geese. A billboard display near the park entrance explains the geology and ecology of this unique lagoon.

Rabbit tunnels riddle the sandy hillside behind the beach, and at dusk the longeared residents appear. Raccoons, too, roam the beaches at night, scavenging

81

for tasty sea creatures. These animals, as well as the local black-tailed deer, can usually be seen during a quiet evening stroll along the beach or park roads.

A log cabin on the end of the spit was recently reconstructed in the original style and on the site of a beach cabin which had been built here more than 50 years ago. Some of the logs are from the original cabin, others were scavenged from the beach. The historic old structure now serves as a picnic shelter.

Less than ½ mile offshore, Flower Island is part of the San Juan Islands Wilderness. While the shores are interesting to explore with canoe or dinghy, do not go ashore, for such intrusion by man disturbs nesting birds.

Frost Island, just a stone's throw from the end of the spit, is privately owned. When boating around these islands in small craft, navigate with care, as the tidal current is strong in the channel.

Trails beginning at the lower campground road climb up the hill to the other camp areas and beyond into the thick timber of the hillside. No views due to the heavy growth, but still a lovely, cool hike on a warm summer day. These trails are primarily fire breaks which terminate at the park boundary.

LOPEZ SOUND

One of the prettiest little cruising corners of the San Juans, with rock-bound islets trimmed with ragged fringes of "bonsai" evergreens, secluded bays, and a narrow pass with a bit of a navigational challenge—just to keep things interesting.

Squeezed between long Lopez Island and the "comma" of Decatur, Lopez Sound is just enough off the beaten path that it does not suit the boater hurriedly

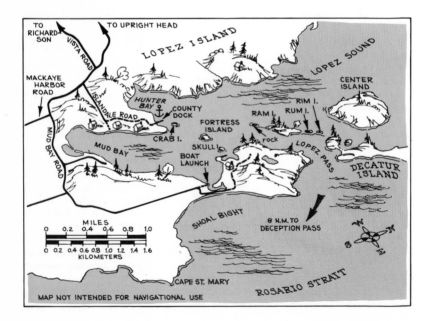

Mud Bay

headed for somewhere else. Instead it attracts cruisers willing to leisurely putt by, inspecting the shoreline, or sailboats looking for a bit of wind.

Fortress, Crab and Skull Islands, between Hunter and Mud Bay, are bird sanctuaries of the San Juan Islands Wilderness; seals can sometimes be seen hauled out on their sunny rocks. The rounded head south of Lopez Pass, joined to the island by a slim neck of land, is a summer youth camp. An authentic Indian dugout canoe belonging to the camp can often be seen drawn up on the shore by the camp, or being paddled in the water of Lopez Sound.

Good anchoring in Hunter Bay, but Mud Bay is quite shallow for that purpose.

At the head of the sound, the Lopez Pass exit is guarded by the protruding reef of Rim, Rum and Ram Islands. Here skippers must continue south 200 feet (60 meters) beyond Ram Island to avoid kelp-flagged rocks, then make a hairpin turn to the left to run the tight little pass into Rosario Strait.

MUD BAY

Portions of the tide flats surrounding Mud Bay are open to the public for clamming and beach exploration. Two boat launches nearby provide put-ins for small boats. The easiest one to reach is on the northeast edge of the bay; to find it follow Ferry Road, then Center Road south from the Upright Head. At an intersection in 8½ miles (13½ km) turn left on Mud Bay Road and follow it south, then east past the head of the bay. Turn left on Sperry Road, heading north; when the main road curves right, a single-lane dirt road continues straight ahead for 300 feet to a turnaround at road end. Here boats may be hand carried the short distance to the water. The nearby lagoon and pebbled beach make interesting exploration by boat or foot.

To reach the second boat launch, follow Mud Bay Road south from the Center Road intersection for about 2 miles (3 km) and turn left (east) on Islandale Road, then left again in another ¾ mile (1 km). Follow the narrow road downhill, avoiding private drives, to the boat ramp and a short county dock on Hunter Bay, just around the point from Mud Bay.

The sheltered waters at the head of Lopez Sound are ideal for paddle adventuring. Bald eagles soaring overhead, nest in the forest nearby. The head of Mud Bay and much of its shore are public tidelands; avoid any property which is posted.

RICHARDSON

Facilities: Fuel, groceries, marine supplies, water, dock, restaurant (at Mackaye Harbor)

Looking directly into the Strait of Juan de Fuca from behind the limited protection of Iceberg Point and offshore islands, Richardson is the southern outpost of the San Juans. At the turn of the century it was one of the major ports of the islands, shipping produce from the farms and orchards of Lopez Island via steamship to Puget Sound markets. A large fishing fleet, comprised of nearly fifty outfits, was based here, unloading their catches at the wharf or taking them directly to mainland canneries.

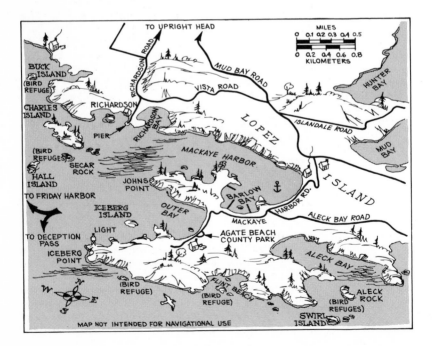

Gillnetter

During this time, it is told, San Juan Channel ran thick with salmon, and at times nets were so full that they could not be lifted into the boats. Today the great runs of fish are depleted and fishermen are fewer and must go farther afield for their catches. Purchasing offices for a cannery are still located on Barlow Bay, at the head of Mackaye Harbor, and gillnetters and purse seniers still raft together in the harbor during fishing season, but the activity does not nearly approximate the days when the harbor bustled with commerce.

Paradoxically, Lopez Island may see the revitalization of the fishing industry, although in a far different way than the hardy fishermen of the 1900s would have envisioned. At Shoal Bay, east of Upright Head on the north end of the island, efforts are being made to raise salmon in pens for sale to commercial markets. Starting with a strain of wild coho, the biologists here are attempting to develop domesticated stock that will flourish despite the stress of captivity. If this pilot venture is successful, and at present it seems to be doing well, it could mean an entirely new method of providing food fish, as well as a boost to the island's economy.

Today Richardson is reduced to a single general store, providing fuel and supplies to commercial fishermen and an occasional pleasure boater. When entering Mackaye Harbor be wary of many rocks around Charles Island, and be forewarned that there is no float, only a stationary pier—crew members may be needed on hand to fend off shiny fiberglass from creosoted pilings. When the straits are kicking up a bit, strong surges can make docking difficult.

Richardson lies 12 nautical miles across Rosario Strait, west of Deception Pass, and 9 nautical miles southwest of Friday Harbor, via San Juan Channel.

Good anchorages can be had at the east end of the harbor and at Barlow Bay. An inn at the head of Mackaye Harbor provides fine meals for boaters tired of galley food; the construction of docks and moorage floats for transient boaters is planned for the near future.

To reach Richardson by land, follow Ferry Road, then Center Road south from the ferry landing. In about 8½ miles (13½ km), where Center Road ends at a T intersection, turn right, then in ¼ mile (⅓ km) left onto Richardson Road; total distance is about 10½ miles (17 km).

The tour down-island is a pleasure for bicyclists, with gently rolling black-topped roads passing neat farms and pastures filled with cattle. Birds call from hedgerow and marsh and the ubiquitous San Juan rabbit dashes across the road—perhaps just a breath ahead of a hawk. Watch for eagles soaring above the range of low hills to the east.

AGATE BEACH PICNIC AREA

Park Area: 1 acre
Facilities: Picnic tables, pit toilets, no water. Day use only
Attractions: Beachcombing

Nothing pretentious, but a welcome resting spot and a lovely beach to walk. To reach the park, turn east onto Vista Road ¼ mile (⅓ km) north of Richardson and follow it for 1¼ miles (2 km) to its intersection with Mud Bay Road. Turn right (south) onto Mud Bay Road, then leave it in 1 mile (1½ km), turning right again onto Mackaye Harbor Road, which circles the shore of the harbor, crosses a neck of land, then contours Outer Bay. The small, grassy picnic area is located near the middle of the beach, on the east side of the road.

Across from the picnic area a stairway descends to the pebbled beach on Outer Bay, facing out to the "toe" of distant San Juan Island. Lying just offshore a smooth rock beckons to kayak explorers. Perhaps it can be reached on foot at low tide. What else does low tide bring? Agates? Crabs? Stop and find out.

ICEBERG POINT AND POINT COLVILLE

Two stretches of land on the far recesses of Lopez Island are held by the Bureau of Land Management as lighthouse reservations. Iceberg Point does house a navigational beacon; Point Colville does not.

At present these two areas can be reached only by boat; land access is closed.

The shorelines beneath the points are extremely rugged. The difficulty of landing boats varies with the tide level and the turbulence of the water. A nice tide flat extends on the south side of Iceberg Point, ringed by steep cliffs—a gorgeous place on a calm day.

WILDERNESS AREA ISLANDS

More than two dozen barren rocks and islets lifting out of the sea off the tip of Lopez Island have been set aside for wildlife management. These bits of rock, along with numerous others located throughout the San Juans, with a total of 352 acres at eighty-four distinct locations, comprise the San Juan Islands Wilderness, administered by the U.S. Fish and Wildlife Service.

Agate Beach County Park

Islands holding this status in the vicinity of Lopez Island, are Shark Reef, located on the west of Lopez near San Juan Island's Cattle Point; Buck Island and Mummy Rocks near Davis Bay; Secar Rock and Hall Island south of Richardson; Aleck Rocks and Swirl Island south of Aleck Bay; 9-acre Castle Island and 11-acre Colville Island (the largest of the bird refuges in the vicinity), off Point Colville; Boulder Island east of Watmough Head; Crab, Fortress and Skull Islands in Lopez Sound; and numerous other small, unnamed rocks.

The sanctuaries were established primarily to protect nesting sea birds. They are also important as resting areas for seals and sea lions, and these pelagic mammals, as well as dolphins and whales forage in surrounding waters.

Glaucous-winged gulls, cormorants, tufted puffins, murres, pigeon guillemots, auklets and black oystercatchers nest in large numbers on the islands, while nearly 200 other species of sea birds are known to stop here during their migration on the Pacific Flyway.

It is well established that the numbers of these birds have dramatically diminished in last century; civilization is almost totally responsible. In early days Indians looted the rookeries for eggs and killed the birds for food and for their decorative value. The parrot-like beaks of tufted puffins were valued for ceremonial rattles and as adornment, and large numbers were killed just for that purpose. Despite this predation, the great flocks survived.

Ruddy turnstones resting on offshore rocks

Today man threatens the existence of these birds with subtler methods; he preempts their habitat, depletes their food sources and poisons their environment. Aside from the moral and æsthetic issues raised by the loss of huge numbers of birds, this tinkering with one of the important links of the food chain must ultimately affect man, too.

These scattered, inhospitable rocks, swept by heavy seas from the Strait of Juan de Fuca, rarely attract recreational boaters; however, the area is growing in popularity with scuba divers. At this time their numbers are small enough so they do not constitute a serious problem; increased activity could seriously disrupt the rookeries. The presence of humans also prevents seals and sea lions from hauling out on the rocks to rest and warm themselves, a necessary function for these animals.

Boaters and fishermen in the area are urged to stay at least 300 feet away from the wilderness area islands to avoid disturbing seals and nesting birds. Discharge of firearms is, of course, prohibited.

Common murre

E. THE CENTRAL CHANNEL

Splitting the San Juans from east to west, a central waterway comprised of Harney Channel and Wasp Passage forms a saltwater freeway used by most boats traveling in the islands. Broad and deep throughout most of its length, the channel is constricted only at its western end where a capricious architect of the sea dumped a load of rocks known as the Wasp Islands.

On this sheltered waterway the ferry makes three of its four island stops to discharge passengers. From the heights of the ferry, tourists look down onto everyone's dream of a vacation retreat—private little islands and points and bays, each decorated with a summer cabin or retirement home, a bit of a dock and a bobbing sailboat.

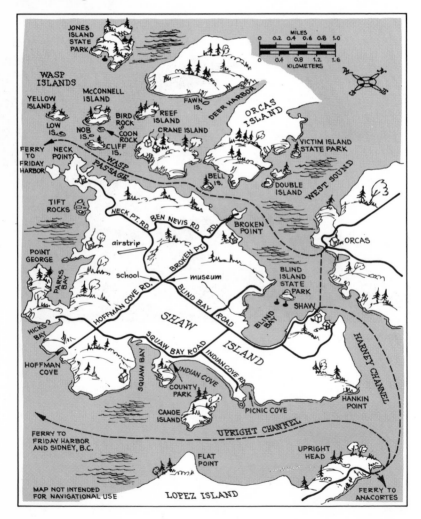

Ferry in Wasp Passage; Shaw Island in foreground and left, Bell Island immediately above ferry and Crane Island just beyond

SHAW ISLAND

Smallest of the islands served by the ferries, Shaw Island has a population of only around a hundred permanent residents on its 4,937 acres. Its sole "commercial" development is the combination general store/post office/ferry terminal/gas station/dock at the ferry landing. The paucity of water on these rocky acres has limited real estate development, and most Shaw Islanders like it that way.

On the southern end of the island, land surrounding Parks Bay and all of Point George is held by the University of Washington's Friday Harbor Laboratories as a biological preserve. Property here has been donated, purchased or leased in order to maintain the shores and uplands in a nearly natural condition for research and educational purposes. Parks Bay is an excellent anchorage, and the tidelands up to the mean high tide level are open for public clamming and oyster picking.

Most island roads are inland, with few views of San Juan waters, and no access to bays. Instead, the roads roll gently through heavy timber and past small fields edged by hedgerows filled with birds and bunnies. Here are not the wide agricultural expanses of Lopez Island, but instead small acreages with a few cattle and crops. Hike or bike the byways and enjoy the catharsis of rural island life.

E. THE CENTRAL CHANNEL

The most scenic street on the island is the one following the west shore of
Blind Bay, with views across the bay to Orcas Island; it dead ends at private
property.

The main "point of interest" is near the center of the island at the intersection
of Blind Bay Road and Hoffman Cove Road, where a classic one-room school
house stands. Known as the "Little Red Schoolhouse", the building is on the
National Register of Historic Places. In 1977 its student enrollment was three.

Across the road is the island's library and historical society, with a reef netting
boat on display on the lawn. The small library and historical collection are open
to the public on Mondays and Saturdays.

Arrive on a morning ferry and spend the day on the island, but plan to leave on
an evening boat unless you are one of the fortunate to be able to claim one of the
eight campsites in the county park or have a good friend on the island. There is
no other place to park a camper or pitch a tent, and there are no motels or cabins.

East of the ferry landing, a small dock with float provides service to visiting
boaters; a few overnight moorages are available.

BLIND ISLAND STATE PARK

Park Area: 2 acres
Access: Boat only
Facilities: Campsite, picnic table, pit toilet, mooring buoys, *no water*
Attractions: Beachcombing, fishing, shrimp

This 2-acre rock, stuck in the entrance to Blind Bay boasts only limited public
facilities, a couple of tenacious trees—and an unparalleled nighttime spectacle!

Blind Island State Park

After sunset, ferries ablaze with lights ply Harney Channel, stopping at times at Shaw and Orcas. Small craft cruise by, resembling nautical fireflies, their reflections glimmering in the darkened sea.

On the south side of the rocky island, four buoys give moorage to boaters, although in rough weather better anchorages can be found farther into the bay. Rocks around the island and in the channel are a navigational hazard.

Hand carried boats may be put in at the ferry landing at Shaw, ¼ nautical mile away, or at Orcas ¾ nautical mile across Harney Channel. Boating traffic is usually heavy in the channel and can present a danger to small boats. Bring a sleeping bag and stay overnight to watch the evening show.

SHAW ISLAND COUNTY PARK

Park Area: 64 acres
Access: Ferry or boat
Faciliites: Campsites, pit toilets, picnic tables, fireplaces, picnic shelter, water, launching ramp
Attractions: Beachcombing, hiking, clams, crabs, swimming, fishing

Facing on Indian Cove, Shaw Island County Park encompasses 65 acres of prime Shaw Island real estate and one of the best sandy beaches in any of the San Juans. The land, once a military reservation, was purchased by Shaw Islanders for public use. Express your gratitude to these far-sighted residents by observing posted regulations and respecting private property bounding the park.

To reach the park from the ferry landing, follow Blind Bay Road, which heads south, and then curves westward, to an intersection with Squaw Bay Road in 1½ miles (2½ km). Turn left (south); in ½ mile (¾ km) more, signs point left to the park's picnic area, or straight ahead to the campground loop.

The day-use picnic area is located above the shore of Indian Cove. A surfaced ramp at the end of the entrance road on the east side of the park provides launching for trailered boats.

Up the road, away from the beach, the campground contains eight spacious sites for the fortunate few and don't ask for more—the fragile ecology of the area cannot tolerate the intrusion of hordes of tourists.

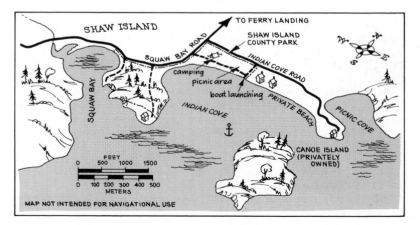

E. THE CENTRAL CHANNEL

Ferry and reef netters in Upright Channel as seen from Shaw Island County Park; Lopez Island and Olympic Mountains in distance

Indian Cove lies just 3½ nautical miles east of Friday Harbor, where boats may be rented. Small boats are easily beached on the shore; deep keel vessels will have to anchor well out in the bay as it is extremely shallow.

The protected, sandy beach slopes gradually outward for several hundred feet. Sand dollars and heart cockles lie near the surface; dig deeper to find more tender clams, and perhaps even the mighty geoduck. On hot summer days the water of the bay warms enough for wading and swimming.

A forested thumb of land on the west, which separates Indian Cove from Squaw Bay is also part of the park. Tides permitting, circumnavigate the peninsula on sandy beaches which turn to rock as they round the point. Squaw Bay, which nearly drains at low tide, is a delightful place for mucking about and observing intertidal life.

On the east side of the peninsula, a dirt road goes through forest to reach the privately owned tip of the island, where a summer home is located; do not trespass. The road is pleasant enough, but with few views and no beach access.

A single-track road on the west side of the peninsula is more attractive. Although it is driveable, it is more fun to park at the road junction and stroll along the embankment, enjoying the gentle murmur of the forest and views of Squaw Cove. At roads end a trail continues less than 50 feet beyond to two tiny coves, embraced by overhanging madronas.

No overnight camping here, and no fires; just peaceful forest, beach and water to enjoy by day.

REEF NETTERS

Commercial reef netting fishing boats can often be seen from Shaw Island County Park working in Upright Channel between Shaw and Lopez Islands. This unique fishing method was originated long ago by Indians in the San Juans, who used dugout canoes and nets fashioned from thin strips of willow or cedar bark.

Pioneers adopted the method, and its use has continued to the present time, only being updated by the use of skiffs or barges with outboard motors, modern nets of synthetic materials and powered winches to haul in the catch.

Reef netting, which is most commonly utilized for sockeye and humpback salmon, employs the use of two boats with high, ladder-like lookout towers in the bow. These boats are anchored 50 feet apart in shallow water or around reefs, with a 50-foot square net stretched between them and weighted down at the bottom. When the lookouts spot a school of fish swimming into the net, it is quickly pulled up and the catch dumped into holding nets. Very clear water, such as is found in the San Juans, is necessary for this fishing method.

THE WASP ISLANDS

Passengers on the inter-island runs are treated to a close-up view of the Wasp Islands as the ferries squeeze through narrow Wasp Passage. Indeed, during fog or heavy storms the view may seem *too* close for the faint-of-heart. Larger ferries which do not stop at Shaw and Orcas avoid the channel by making an end-run around Shaw Island through Upright Channel to Friday Harbor.

Reef netters on beach at Shaw Island County Park

Boneparte's gulls

This group of assorted islets and rocks, known to ferry captains as "the Rock Pile", received its name, not from the pernicious insect, but from the American warship, Wasp, which distinguished itself during the War of 1812. Jones Island to the north, was named for its commander, Jacob Jones.

Early pioneers frequently rowed sheep to these small islands for summer grazing, and since most are dry, it was also necessary to regularly haul over barrels of drinking water for the flocks.

Much of the colorful history of the San Juans, when pirates and smugglers frequented these waters, centers around the Wasp Islands. McConnell Island was the family home of Victor McConnell, one of these early day racketeers—until his relatives discovered his activities and requested his absence.

In the late 1880s, the U.S. closed its doors to Chinese immigrants eager for jobs in this bountiful nation, and smuggling of these aliens, who had made their way from their homeland to Canada, became a lucrative profession. Along with them came cargoes of heavily-taxed opium (which was legal at the time), silk and other commodities. A few years later when imported wool was slapped with a stiff duty, enterprising boats slipped north to Canada to purchase fleece which could be mixed with the San Juan product and innocently resold, causing revenuers to wonder at the productivity of island sheep.

When Washington state went "dry" in 1916, 4 years before the Volstead Act decreed nation-wide Prohibition, the smuggling flotilla heeded the cry of the thirsty, and dutifully swung into action, importing everything from fine, bonded Canadian whiskey to watered-down rotgut from the stills of willing northern neighbors.

The San Juan Archipelago is ideally suited to such clandestine activities, with its maze of channels spotted with rocky hiding places and soupy fogs clinging about the shoulders of the islands. Local sailors in small, fast-moving craft knew every inch of the waterways and every trick-of-the-trade. One favorite ploy was to slip on the lee side of a ferry and sneak by under the very noses of watchful revenue boats.

Romantic as it may sound, smuggling was not an innocent pastime, for these were days of undercover agents, hijackings, bloody shoot-outs, mysterious

Yellow Island, one of the Wasp Group

disappearances of crews and boats and blatant murders. Frequently cargoes were hurriedly "deep-sixed" by smugglers fearing apprehension. At least one instance is reported of Chinese aliens being forced overboard; their bodies, with hands and feet bound, later washed up on nearby shores.

Charged with the enforcement of Prohibition, the Coast Guard with its larger, slower-moving boats, was hard-pressed to apprehend the elusive rumrunners. However, the government boats knew a few tricks, too, and one skipper in particular, Lorenz A. Lonsdale, captain of the tug *Arcata,* gave such good account of himself that he was in constant danger of being relieved of command and "kicked upstairs" by pressure exerted by corrupt politicians, dismayed by his successes.

Life today is much more sedate along this central channel. Instead of woolly flocks, the islands are dotted with summer homes—although it is still necessary to import water to many of their occupants. On foggy mornings it is easy to imagine ghosts of early smugglers slipping furtively past the mist-cloaked shores.

Crane Island, with many private residences on its 222 wooded acres, is the largest and most developed of the Wasp group. San Juan Airlines regularly stops on the airstrip in the center of the island to provide transportation and deliver supplies to island residents.

Smaller Bell Island to the east and Cliff, Coon, McConnell, Yellow and Reef Islands scattered to the west are singly-owned, with one or two summer hide-aways on each. Down the scale of "ownership", the barren, inhospitable rocks which cannot even support a shack are given over to the sea birds and seals. Bird Rock, east of McConnell Island, the Nob Island group and Low Island west of Cliff Island and an unnamed low-tide rock west of Yellow Island are all part of the San Juan Islands Wilderness.

Boaters enjoy exploring the watery nooks and crannies of the Wasp Islands; however, extreme care must be used for there are many submerged rocks and reefs. Kelp marks many of these danger spots, but a slow speed and a vigilant eye on the navigational chart are the pilot's best allies. Smaller, unpowered boats should also be wary of wakes from the ferry and other boating traffic.

E. THE CENTRAL CHANNEL

JONES ISLAND

Area: 188 acres
Access: Boat only
Facilities: Float, mooring buoys, campsites, picnic tables, fireplaces, water
  (well frequently goes dry)
Attractions: Beachcombing, clams, crabs, abalone, fishing, hiking, skin diving

A choice little island with welcoming bays and bountiful shores, located so near the main highways of Wasp Passage and San Juan Channel that most passing tourists drop in for a brief visit—and many fall in love and linger awhile.

Jones Island is located less then ½ mile off the southwest tip of Orcas Island, and 2 nautical miles from Deer Harbor Marina, the nearest point where boats can be launched. Boaters approaching Jones Island through Spring Passage should be cautious of several rocky shoals just off the east shore.

A cove deeply notching the north side of the island holds a dock with float and a few mooring buoys. On nice summer weekends this bay is always filled with small boats drawn up on the beach and larger ones tied to the float, rafted together on buoys, or bobbing on a hook.

Anchoring in this bay can be tricky, especially with a bit of wind or a strong tidal current to complicate matters. The bottom is rocky and steeply sloping, making it difficult to set a hook solidly. Savvy seamen will often drop a second anchor or will row a stern line ashore and tie up to a tree to keep their craft in position. If unsure about the security of your anchor or that of nearby boats, do not leave your boat unattended. A favorite pastime among those familiar with the bay is sitting on deck with the air of an "old salt" (once one's own boat is solidly nailed down), and watching the embarrassment of the uninitiated as they drift on their anchors.

On the south side of the island is a wider, shallower bay, split by a rocky headland. The three additional buoys placed here are more open to tossing by wind and waves.

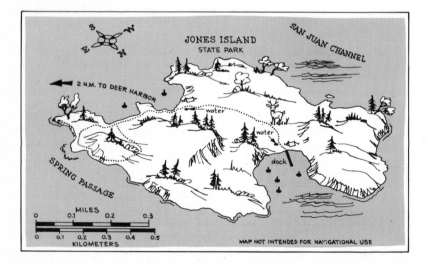

98   **Early morning at Jones Island State Park**

E. THE CENTRAL CHANNEL

Deer at Jones Island State Park

The park attracts many visitors in small boats who overnight ashore in the campgrounds overlooking the two bays. Campsites, picnic tables and fireplaces at the north cove are clustered in cool timber; on the south bay a large grassy meadow offers sunnier sites and views of the Wasp Islands.

Crossing the narrow waist of the island, a ½ mile trail connects the two anchorages. At the approach of a low tide, boaters traipse southward along this path, armed with shovels and buckets, headed for the clam beds on the far shore. Even without the incentive of clams, visitors will enjoy the forest walk through the deep green of the island's interior. Cedar, hemlock, swordfern and salal suddenly give way to the warm golden meadow on the south bay.

A small herd of black-tailed deer which inhabit the island often graze in this meadow. Raccoons, weasels and martens, who are occasionally spotted at dusk by hikers, swim across Spring Passage to raid the nests of sea birds and some of the bolder raccoons also check out the garbage cans by the campgrounds.

Several sketchy trails circle eastward on low bluffs looking down into little one-boat bays facing on Spring Passage. Use care scrambling about on the rocky embankment, as footing can be insecure; hikers have been injured here.

The west shore, at the edge of San Juan Channel, is a favorite spot for salmon fishermen. Prized abalone which cling to the rocky western skirts of the island are harvested by skin divers or can be pried off the rocks by beachcombers during low, low tide. Dungeness crab, which migrate around the island at some primitive whim, can sometimes be trapped in the south bay.

As of 1978, Jones Island was owned by the federal government as a part of the San Juan Islands National Wildlife Refuge, and leased by the state for use as a

Jones Island beach and Spring Passage

marine park. Since the throngs of people using the island are not particularly compatible with its wildlife status, in the future the U.S. Fish and Wildlife Service may relinquish its claim and turn it over to the state in return for several smaller, more remote, state-owned islands.

Jones Island, in a microcosm, reflects many of the problems besetting the San Juans as a whole. With its many attractions and convenient location, it may ultimately be "loved to death" by the squadrons of boaters who arrive on its shores in greater numbers each year.

Today ignorant visitors scar campgrounds by "ditching" their tents, injure trees with nails driven to support tent ropes, strip branches from anything green to fuel their campfires, pockmark the beaches and shore with randomly built bonfires (and also risk setting the entire island ablaze), trample undergrowth by careless hiking, frighten the wildlife and kill or cart away even the inedible living beach creatures. Even the well-intentioned camper who treats the land with care, simply by his presence has a negative impact on the environment. The space requirements and waste disposal logistics of tens of thousands of visitors creates problems which must be dealt with.

As with all of the San Juans, Jones Island simply cannot tolerate the pressures of unlimited use and abuse by demanding recreationists. Without careful development and management and sensitive, responsible use, the future may well see its beaches stripped naked, its meadows ground to dust, its forest destroyed and its wildlife departed.

F. SAN JUAN ISLAND

Verdant, pastoral country, punctuated by forested mountains—most populated of the islands—home of the county seat and its largest (and only incorporated) town—center of commerce and industry—home port for the local commercial fishing fleet—crossroads of these boundary waters, with a steady flow of international traffic through its two customs offices. The archipelago's busiest island.

Yet "busy" is a relative term in this slow-paced paradise. Even in summer, when tourists stream from crammed-full ferries, and harbors and bays swarm with boats, the customary tempo only slightly quickens. Many visitors, understanding the ambience of the island, arrive on bicycles or on foot with backpack, prepared to enjoy the country at a leisurely rate.

Early explorers noted the important strategic location of the island facing on two major waterways, and its outstanding physical features, and named it San Juan, principal landfall of this group. Arriving later, British settlers who claimed it for the Queen changed its name to Bellevue Island, but eventually the original Spanish designation was restored.

Pioneers recognized San Juan as prime real estate, with its gently rolling farm land ideal for cattle and crops, its thick forests ripe to be turned into cabins, barns, fences and firewood, and its fine harbors providing sheltered access to the shores. Generation after generation they sank their family roots into the island soil.

Today's new San Juan settlers are retirees, artists, authors and dropouts from the rat race who prefer their air without smog, their beaches without pollution-slicks and beer cans, their highways without traffic jams, and their starry nights without obliterating city lights.

The island can be reached by Washington State ferry from Anacortes or Sidney, B.C. to Friday Harbor, about a 1½-hour trip either way. For quicker access, San Juan Airlines has regularly scheduled flights from Seattle and Bellingham to the airports at Friday Harbor and Roche Harbor. All plane stops are made only by prior reservation.

Private boats visiting the island will find transient moorage and supplies at Friday Harbor and at resorts on Roche Harbor and Mitchell Bay. Numerous fine anchorages are found around the island, as described in the following text, however public access is limited.

Hikers and cyclists will enjoy the gently rolling roads edged by pastures and forest, sometimes dropping down to round a salty bay, other times skirting the edge of a bluff, offering marine panoramas. Nearly all roads are two-lane blacktop with very little shoulder, but traffic moves at a relaxed pace, and traveling the roads is quite safe if simple precautions are observed.

Virtually all facilities and services which are to be found on San Juan Island are located at Friday Harbor. Small stores at Roche Harbor and Mitchell Bay pump fuel and carry supplies for campers, boaters and fishermen, but the selection is limited.

A handful of resorts, hotels and motels at Friday Harbor and at a few other locations on the north end of the island provide overnight accommodations by day or week, ranging from modern motels to rustic beach cabins. Advanced reservations are essential in summer.

Jakel's Lagoon

F. SAN JUAN ISLAND

Purse seiners at Friday Harbor

In addition to the county campground at Smallpox Bay, camping facilities are available at a commercial campground near Friday Harbor and at several of the marine resorts. Some will make reservations; call for current information. Parking or tenting overnight along the road is not permitted.

FRIDAY HARBOR

Access: Ferry, boat or airplane
Facilities: Groceries, stores, fuel, marine repair, boat launching, boat rental and charters, dock with water and electrical hookups, hotels, restaurants, U.S. Customs, restrooms, showers, laundry
Attractions: Boating, fishing, shopping, sightseeing, marine laboratories

An enchanting mix of old and new establishments, some "shopping center modern", some elderly but beautifully renovated, still others nostagically decrepit—all with a dash of salt thrown in. Shopping facilities are within walking distance of the ferry landing and public dock. Grocery stores provide delivery service to boats on the docks, fine restaurants cater to tourists, galleries offer quality work of local artists and craftsmen while other shops have selections of souvenirs and gifts for the folks back home.

Ferries from Anacortes and Sidney arrive regularly during the day to disgorge their passengers, their window-rattling whistle blasts barely noted by local residents. Sometimes two of the green and white behemoths are in the harbor, one patiently treading water in the outer bay, awaiting its turn at the slip.

Friday Harbor is virtually a nautical "Times Square" of the Northwest—stand there long enough and eventually every cruising boat that you know will pass by. In 1977 the public dock hosted nearly 10,000 transient boats, double the amount for 1973. Approximately 120 visiting boats can tie up each night, with some rafting and doubling up; more dock space is planned for the future.

The port also has over 150 permanent moorages. If unable to find overnight space in the visitor's floats, check with the dock office for available moorages. Frequently local boats are out for a time and will sublet their slips. Do not tie up in a permanent moorage without permission from the dock office. If unable to secure a space, the bay northwest of the docks provides anchorages within dinghy range of the floats.

The building at the head of the dock complex houses the harbormaster and U.S. Customs offices and restrooms and showers for the use of visiting mariners.

Even non-sailors will enjoy a stroll down the floats to admire, and perhaps envy, the many boats, some from exotic hailing ports. The commercial fishing

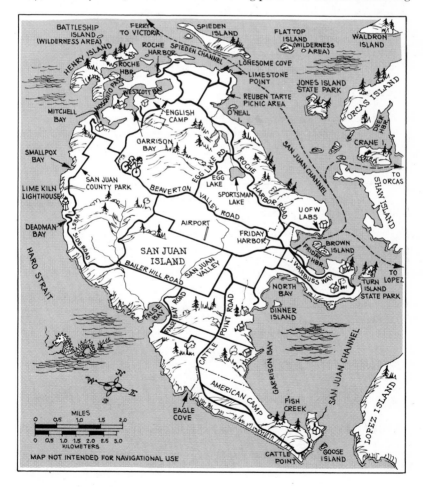

fleet ties up on the larger docks—gillnetters and purse-seiners with huge, stern-mounted metal spools rolled fat with nets.

In the water, like ghostly Mary Poppinses, hundreds upon hundreds of hydroid jellyfish rise and descend and drift around the pilings. Researchers at the University of Washington's Friday Harbor Laboratories harvest thousands of these jellyfish each year to be processed into Aequorin, an important substance with bioluminescent properties which is used in medical research.

At low tide, dock pilings reveal underwater coatings of fluffy sea anemones, feather duster worms, opalescent nudibranches and spidery decorator crabs who glue bits of seaweed to their bodies as protective camouflage.

WHALE MUSEUM

A recent addition to the Friday Harbor scene is a whale museum, featuring interesting displays on these great mammals. Actual whale skeletons and life-sized models fill the hall, while murals and other displays give further information.

The whale museum is located at 1st and Court Streets, three blocks from the ferry terminal. To find it, go south on Spring Street to 1st, then right two blocks to Court. The museum is housed on the second floor of the Odd Fellows Hall.

SEEING WHALES

Whale sightings are certainly one of the most thrilling experiences of the San Juans, and one that is not reserved for boaters alone, for pods of whales have been seen from land and even from the ferry. At such times ferry captains have been known to slow their engines and alert passengers.

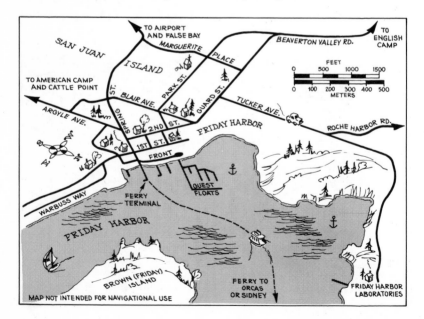

Orca

A "sighting" may consist of only a momentary revelation—a fish flinging itself out of the grayness of the sea, twisting frantically, then dropping back into the water, to be followed by a boat-sized curving back, displaying a 5-foot-high triangular fin which is gone as quickly as the small fish.

At other times a ruffling of the surface of the water is noticed, then it is suddenly filled with several great black bodies slashed with white, surfacing and blowing for several minutes, which may then disappear and reappear a quarter of a mile away. Porpoises (which are toothed whales, as are orcas), have been known to follow in the wake of power boats—skippers are startled to look back and find them there.

The most common whale sighted in the island is the "killer whale", *Orcinis orca*, or orca as it is more correctly called. Northwest Indians considered the orca to be "the wolf of the sea", for working in highly organized packs they are swift, efficient predators of schools of fish, dolphins and even larger whales. Bad press to the contrary, however, there has not been one authenticated attack by orcas on humans, and when captured by man they display gentle, friendly, intelligent behavior.

Several other species of whales are sometimes seen in the inland waters. Minke and gray whales (both baleen whales) are often larger than orcas. Smaller pilot whales (black fish), harbor porpoises and Dall porpoises are also frequently spotted. Dalls are also black with white markings, but only orcas display the striking white underbelly, reaching from jaw to near the tail, the great fin, from 3 to 5 feet tall, and the awesome 20 to 30 foot length.

F.   SAN JUAN ISLAND

At the turn of the century, settlers reported regular sightings of great pods of whales containing more than a hundred individuals. Although these reports perhaps were exaggerated, there is no doubt that there once were far more whales than there are today. It is believed that there are four pods, totaling about seventy individuals are now residents of the inland waters.

While whale sightings are not commonplace in the San Juans, neither are they rare. The Moclips Cetological Society, under contract to the U.S. National Marine Fisheries Service is engaged in cataloging all whale sightings in the islands, Straits of Juan de Fuca and Puget Sound, in order to attempt to identify them and chart their movements.

Any whale sightings should be reported to the Orca Survey at 1-(800)-562-8832. Information on sightings should include time and location, direction of movement of the whales, numbers sighted and, if possible, the type of whale.

It is illegal to harass or pursue with a boat any marine mammal. If whales are sighted, they should be observed at a distance and at a slow speed. Boaters are far more likely to be able to observe a pod for a length of time if they stay at a distance and do not appear to be a threat.

UNIVERSITY OF WASHINGTON FRIDAY HARBOR LABORATORIES

With shorelines ranging from quiet bays and saltwater lagoons to rocky shelves swept by swift-flowing tides, the San Juan Archipelago provides an exceptional opportunity for marine research. Tidal fluctuations of nearly 12 feet expose vast tidelands harboring specimens of many diverse marine plant and invertebrate species.

Recognizing the unique character of the archipelago, the University of Washington established a marine biology research center on San Juan Island in 1904. When land from a former military preserve at Friday Harbor became available, the Laboratories moved onto the 484-acre tract, there growing to become a fine educational and research facility, attracting visiting scientists from all over the world.

Ferries arriving at Friday Harbor pass the attractive campus on the north shore of the outer harbor. A modern-day aqueduct can be seen snaking along the bank; fashioned of polyethlene, the pipes deliver contaminant-free sea water to laboratory aquaria.

The Laboratories are open to visitors through July and August on Wednesdays and Saturdays from 2 to 4 p.m. Guides show visitors through some of the buildings and answer questions regarding the facilities, the research and educational programs and the specimens which are on display.

To reach the campus from Friday Harbor, travel west from the ferry dock on Spring Street to Second Street. Turn right, then in three blocks turn left on Guard. After one more block turn right on Tucker, which shortly becomes Roche Harbor Road. The signed turnoff is on the right, 1 mile (1½ km) from the ferry terminal. Since the Laboratories are located on a carefully protected biological preserve, pets must remain in cars or be kept on a leash at all times.

The University of Washington also administers biological preserves at several other areas in the San Juans. These islands have been donated, purchased or leased to protect them in a nearly natural state for research and educational purposes. The largest of these holdings is on Shaw Island, and includes most of

Display pool at Friday Harbor Laboratories

Left: Moon snail — found on sandy beaches in the San Juans. Right: sand collar, the egg case of the moon snail

the land and shoreline extending from Point George to Squaw Bay; others are at False Bay on San Juan Island and Iceberg Point and Point Colville on the southern end of Lopez Island.

In an effort to protect marine lands, all of the seashores and seabed of San Juan County and around Cypress Island in Skagit County are designated a marine biological preserve. Areas with this status are open for public recreation, but Washington State law prohibits the taking or destruction of any living specimen, except for food use, without the written permission of the Director of the Friday Harbor Laboratories.

Intertidal lands are vast displays of marine life, where can be observed the competition and predation of these animals and their peculiar adaptations for survival. Delicate interrelationships are easily disrupted by public misuse, and over-collecting of any particular species, even the natural predators such as starfish, can have far-reaching effects on the overall marine balance (in addition to being unlawful).

Especially sensitive are very slow-growing species which must not be harvested in quantity due to their long replacement cycle. While the edible mussel is fast-growing and readily replaces itself, the California mussel, larger, with a rougher, ribbed shell, is much slower to replace itself in chilly Northwest waters. Goose barnacles, which are sometimes gathered for food, are also slow-growing in the San Juans.

Abalone were once rare here, but recently have become quite abundant; overharvesting of this popular food item could seriously deplete their numbers. Scuba divers and fishermen often take rockfish on rocky bottoms near pilings. A rockfish 2 feet long needs 30 years to grow that large, compared to a salmon which will grow to an equal size in 3 to 4 years. It makes a lot of sense to protect large rockfish, since they contribute relatively enormous numbers of young fish to the population annually, in addition to taking a long time to achieve their large size. Taking smaller individuals, e.g. 1 to 3 pounds, has a lesser impact on future generations.

With the increasing scarcity of choice butter clams, oysters and Dungeness crabs, human beach foragers are displaying a greater interest in adding to their gastronomic fare the more bizarre marine forms: leathery chitons, limpets and moon snails and grotesque sea cucumbers and goose barnacles.

The taking for food use of nearly every form of marine life in Washington is controlled by state law. The Department of Fisheries sport fishing pamphlet, available in most sporting goods stores, lists bag limits and other restrictions.

TURN ISLAND

Park Area: 35 acres
Access: Boat only
Facilities: Mooring buoys, campsites, picnic tables, stoves, pit toilets, *no water*
Attractions: Beachcombing, hiking, clams, crabs, mussels, tide pools, scuba
  diving

Situated so near the boating throngs at Friday Harbor, Turn Island receives considerable use, especially by boaters with small craft that can be beached on the island's inviting shores. In summer the campsites are frequently full, although the lack of drinking water precludes an extended stay.

In good weather even row boats can manage the excursion through Friday Harbor and along the shores of San Juan Island to the park. En route, view the many gracious homes lining the shores on San Juan and Brown Islands. Total distance is less than 2 nautical miles, all of it near land.

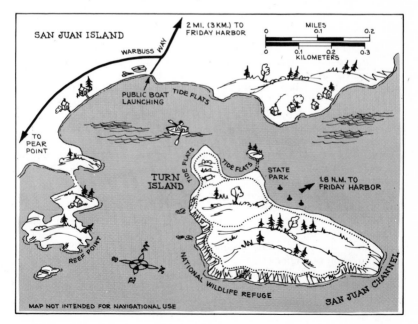

Deer swimming between islands in the San Juans

Small boats may also be put in at a public launching area just spitting distance from Turn Island. To reach it by car, follow Harrison, a one-way street heading east along the shore of Friday Harbor. In a few blocks Harrison joins Warbuss Way, which can be followed to the signed public launch area, about 2 miles from Friday Harbor. The island park lies only ¼ mile across the channel.

Turn Island is under joint jurisdiction—being owned by the federal government as part of the San Juan Islands National Wildlife Refuge, and also managed cooperatively by the state for public recreational use as a marine state park. In the near future the U.S. Fish and Wildlife Service will clarify its policy concerning such joint usage. Plans are to have a small kiosk near the beach to give information and regulations regarding public use.

The best anchorages are found on the west side of the island, where there are three buoys. Moorages here are only slightly sheltered by the landmasses and can be quite uncomfortable in a stiff northerly; at other times they promise a pleasant night's stay.

Scattered about the gentle beaches on the southwest end of the island, numerous campsites offer a variety of views: north to San Juan Channel, west to nearby San Juan Island, or east to Lopez Island.

At low tide, this end of the island becomes a great, big tide flat, with clams and mussels awaiting harvesting. Tide pools are exposed at low, low water, or they can be observed by floating in a dinghy just offshore and gazing down into the water at the dazzling undersea world of marine life—brilliant purples, oranges and reds, pastel pinks, greens and lavenders; the color range is limitless. Polarized sun glasses reduce glare on the water and make viewing much easier. The shallow water is excellent for snorkeling.

A 300-yard path cuts across the middle of the island, connecting the main camping area with a pretty beach on the far side. Encircling the island, another connecting trail invites a pleasant 1-mile (1½ km) tramp through light timber, looking out to busy San Juan Channel.

Near the northeast end, Turn Rock, with its navigational beacon, can be seen just offshore. The island and rock are so named because they mark the point where vessels must turn in the channel. The rock is another of the animal sanctuaries of the San Juan Islands Wilderness.

The northeast side of the island is quite precipitous; beaches around the rest of the island are easily reached from the trail above.

Rabbits, raccoon and other small mammals inhabit Turn Island, along with black-tailed deer. These deer, which can be found throughout the San Juans, swim from island to island, sometimes across extremely broad and swift-flowing channels.

Turn Island at one time held a huge bald eagle nest, however the tree supporting the nest recently broke in a storm, destroying it. Reported to have been in continuous use by several generations of eagles for over 70 years, the nest had been abandoned at the time of its destruction. Frequent disturbances by humans can cause the birds to abandon a nesting site, or they may be driven out by infestation of vermin brought to the nest on captured rodents. There are other eagle nesting sites in the vicinity.

SPORTSMAN AND EGG LAKES

Area: Sportsman Lake—87 acres; Egg Lake—6.6 acres
Facilities: Boat launching area, dock on Egg Lake
Attractions: Fishing, bird watching, canoeing

Bird heaven! Cattails and bogs edge open water of two lakes only a few minutes drive from Friday Harbor. Red-winged blackbirds perch sidesaddle on cattails; an array of wild migratory ducks coexist with plump domestic ducks and geese from neighboring farms. During spring mating season, marsh birds loudly advertise their territorial boundaries. All this and fish too!

Sportsman Lake lies to the left of the Roche Harbor Road, 4 miles (6½ km) northwest of Friday Harbor. A short spur road on the northeast side of the lake leads to a gravel boat ramp.

Open to fishing the year around, the 87-acre lake contains largemouth bass and spiny ray. All surrounding lands are private, but no matter, for the beauty lies in the bogs and the birds and the tranquil water. Drop in a boat for fishing, bird watching, or just for a row around the lake.

Sportsman's tiny counterpart, Egg Lake, lies just 300 yards to the west. To reach the lake, continue on the Roche Harbor Road for less than ½ mile (¾ km) to the intersection with Egg Lake Road. Turn left and follow the gravel road for ¾ mile (1 km); through the trees on the left the lake and a small dock can be seen. This is the only public access.

Sportsman Lake boat launch

Egg Lake is regularly planted with trout. Fishing is permitted from April 16 through October 31; gasoline motors are not legal. Aside from the public dock, all bordering lands are private.

A 200-acre commercial campground and recreation area are located just across the Egg Lake Road, north of Egg and Sportsman Lakes. Here, former marshes have been dammed to form a network of private ponds for fishing, swimming and canoeing.

LIMESTONE POINT

Colonies of coral and other sedentary marine animals, growing in the warm waters of an ancient sea, created the typical beds of white limestone which distinctively mark the 80-foot knob of Limestone Point. Summertime boaters hurrying by in Spieden Channel note the attractive shoreline, but few stop to explore its threatening reefs and shoals.

A small resort and campground lie just west of the point at Lonesome Cove and its adjacent Namu's Cove. (This area was the site for the filming of the movie **Namu, the Killer Whale,** thus the name.) The campground is now a favorite with hikers and cyclists.

The underwater walls of the point and the offshore reefs are home for copious amounts of marine life, making the area a favorite with scuba divers, who explore the waters along the channel and southeast around the point.

Rueben Tarte Picnic Area, a primitive public access, is located on a small but very pretty cove southeast of Limestone Point. To reach it, follow Roche Harbor Road for 8 miles (12¾ km) from Friday Harbor, turning right (north) onto Roulleau Road. In another mile turn right again (east) at the intersection with Limestone Road. The road to Lonesome Cove is passed on the left; when the road forks, turn right, now heading south, away from Limestone Point. In about ¼ mile (½ km) watch carefully for a very steep, narrow gravel road going down to the beach. The route is usually not signed and may be difficult to find.

ROCHE HARBOR

Access: Ferry, boat or airplane
Facilities: Transient moorage on docks with water and electrical hookup,
    mooring buoys, boat launching, boat rental, fuel, restrooms, showers,
    laundry, groceries, hotel, restaurant, U.S. Customs
Attractions: Boating, fishing, hiking, scuba diving, swimming pool, sightseeing,
    historical landmarks

   Relics of an earlier, much different time mingle easily with the objects of a
modern-day vacation resort. A hundred-year-old log cabin stands within a few
feet of busy tennis courts and an Olympic-sized swimming pool. Skeletons of a
tug and ferry, remainders of the industrial heyday of the town, moulder on the
beach overlooking the bustle of posh fiberglass cruisers. Visitors register at a
hotel which in the 1850s saw duty as a Hudson's Bay trading post and which later
hosted Presidents Teddy Roosevelt and William Howard Taft.
   To reach Roche Harbor from the Friday Harbor ferry landing, drive west on
Spring Street, turning right on Second Street. In 3 blocks turn left on Guard and
after 1 more block, right on Tucker. At a Y in the road, bear left on Roche Harbor
Road, which continues to the resort, 10¼ miles (16¾ km) from the ferry landing.

Roche Harbor fuel dock

115

F. SAN JUAN ISLAND

The harbor is 11 nautical miles by boat from Friday Harbor and 22 nautical miles from Victoria Harbor on Vancouver Island. In summer the busy docks are a happy mingling of Canadian and Yankee boaters checking in at Customs and stocking up on provisions and fuel before moving on to more remote islands. Old friends are met, new ones are made and sea stories are swapped.

On the week of Dominion Day (July 1st) and the 4th of July, the harbor is even more festive, with fireworks and special events. The evening flag-lowering ceremony, which takes place throughout the summer months, holds special meaning at this time when Canadians and Americans join together in friendship to honor their countries.

The resort may also be reached by private plane, and San Juan Airlines provides regular service to the airfield near the resort.

The historic old hotel and restaurant, graced with a prize-winning formal flower garden, are the center of harbor activity. A display in the lobby of the Hotel de Haro tells of Roche Harbor history. A young Indiana lawyer, John S. McMillin, built the largest lime producing company west of the Mississippi, and for 50 years "ruled" the town. He became one of the richest and most influential men in the state, and even entertained hopes of becoming one of its governors.

After McMillin's death in 1936, his son operated the family business until the lime deposits began to play out. In 1956 the town was sold to its present owner, Rueben Tarte. The lime kilns were shut down shortly thereafter and the Tarte family turned their attention to restoration of the deteriorated buildings and development of a modern resort.

AFTERGLOW VISTA MAUSOLEUM

Forsake the activity of Roche Harbor for a stroll through quiet woods to rub elbows with McMillin family ghosts. From the Hotel de Haro follow the path northwest past the church toward the swimming pool. On the left is a one-room log cabin, believed to have been the home of the Scurr brothers who lived here in the mid-1800s and who sold the property to John S. McMillin.

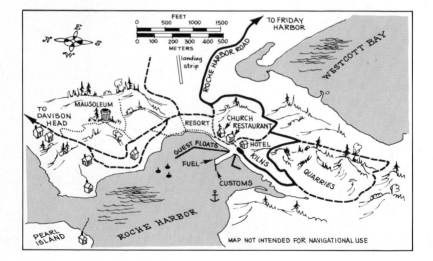

Afterglow Vista Mausoleum

Abandoned lime kiln

Continue on the path until it joins Roche Harbor Road in ¼ mile. Turn left (north) and follow the black-topped road for another ¼ mile to a dirt side road on the right; this road is barred to vehicles, though it is often used by horseback riders and bicyclists. In 200 yards the path reaches the gateway arch of the mausoleum.

Several tiers of stairs lead to a platform encircled with Doric columns. In the center is a round stone table surrounded by six stone chairs. The encroaching forest adds to the erie calm of the spot. It is a privilege to be permitted to visit this unique shrine; please treat it with respect.

John S. McMillan chose this spot for his final resting place because he enjoyed the splendid sunset afterglow on Spieden Channel; however today second-growth timber obscures the view he so prized. The significance of the construction of the tomb is based on the family history and on the Masonic Order, of which McMillin was a member. The intentionally broken column represents life broken by death, while the ring supported by the remaining columns represents the eternal life after death.

The table and chairs are placed just as they were in the family dining room, with McMillin at the head of the table and an open space at the foot facing westward, so that all could enjoy the sunset. The bases of the chairs hold the ashes of the deceased members of the family, who rest here for eternity, their spirits watching the sunset just as they did in life.

For an interesting loop trip and further McMillin history, continue on the trail on the north side of the mausoleum. Switchbacking downhill, the trail drops through lush undergrowth to the road in ¼ mile. An ancient water tank to the left of the trail was part of an extensive water system installed to collect rainwater for Luella McMillin to shampoo her hair.

On the west side of the road, near the point where the trail emerges, are the ruins of Afterglow Manor, the mansion built for McMillin's son, which burned to the ground in 1944. The original stonework is still visible, although overgrown with shrubs and vines. The property is posted as "private—no trespassing"; the stonework can be seen well from the road. Aging stone pillars of the estate entrance still flank the road.

Continue southward; near the swimming pool-tennis court complex watch for trails dropping through the timber to the beach. Here are more antique log cabins, still in use as storage sheds, and the debris of two long-ago wrecked boats. From here walk the beach back to Roche Harbor; total distance of loop hike, 1½ miles (2½ km).

LIME QUARRY

A row of abandoned lime kilns overlook the waters of Roche Harbor. For a closer inspection of the kilns and the quarries which were the life-blood of the town, take a loop hike along the road, pausing to inspect the rusted railroad tracks and machinery, visualizing the quarries at the height of their productivity, when 15,000 barrels of lime per day were turned out.

From the grocery store walk southwest along the road at the water's edge. Immediately to the left are the lime kilns with the gracefully arching brickwork still intact. Continue uphill, following the road left when it turns sharply at the first intersection. Pass gaping quarries where undergrowth is creeping back to gentle the harsh outlines.

Near the top of the hill stop and enjoy a sweeping view of Roche Harbor, Spieden Channel, Mosquito Pass and Henry Island, then the road ducks into timber, briefly losing sight of the harbor. Turn left at the intersection with a blacktopped road, then left again at a driveway which drops steeply downhill past some private homes, headed back to the bay. The driveway deadends at a path which brings the hiker back to the plaza between the hotel and restaurant, a short distance from the grocery store. Total round trip distance, 1¼ miles (2 km).

F. SAN JUAN ISLAND

POSEY ISLAND STATE PARK

Park Area: 1 acre
Access: Boat only
Facilities: Campsite, picnic table, pit toilet, *no water*
Attractions: Beachcombing, fishing, scuba diving, snorkeling, tide pools

A dot of an island just outside Roche Harbor provides a lovely afternoon picnic spot, or in fair weather a campsite with a superb sunset. Posey Island lies less than a nautical mile northeast of Roche Harbor, the nearest place where boats may be launched. Boaters in small craft can take the shorter route through the channel at the east end of Pearl Island, while deeper draft vessels are better advised to stay in the main channel at the west end of Pearl, and anchor well out, as the water surrounding Posey Island is quite shallow and reefs extend out on the north and east. The protected, shallow water makes this an ideal voyage for canoe or kayak.

Due to the fact that the sun sets in the rainy district of Vancouver Island, the San Juans have exceptionally vivid sunsets. The crimson and gold colors, intensified by the black masses of the islands, linger in the sky and sea long after the sun has disappeared. Posey Island, with its open views of Haro Strait and Canadian islands is a prime spot for savoring the afterglow.

THE WEST SIDE

MOSQUITO PASS

Access: Boat only
Facilities (at Snug Harbor): Boat launching, boat rental and charter, cabins, camping, restrooms, groceries
Attractions: Boating, fishing, scuba diving, clams, crabs

A skinny, 1½-mile-long waterway between Henry and San Juan Islands connects Roche Harbor and Westcott, Garrison and Mitchell Bays. The pass and the three shallow bays are ideal for small boat exploration, although tides can be strong and unpredictable in Mosquito Pass itself, where unpowered boats should use great care. Deep keel vessels should not attempt the channel without the aid of charts, for there are many rocks and shoals.

Roche Harbor Resort and the marina on the south side of Mitchell Bay both have launching facilities and rental of small boats.

At low tide clams may be found on many of the sandy beaches of the channel (avoid posted areas); thick beds of eel grass at Nelson Bay and in Mosquito Pass harbor Dungeness crabs.

Resembling a letter "H" crudely scrawled in the water to the west of Mosquito Pass, Henry Island shelters the San Juan bays from waves of Haro Strait. The island rests on the protruding edge of an underwater shelf, and bluffs on the west side plunge steeply downward to a depth of over 120 fathoms. The edge of this shelf, especially the area off Kellett Bluff, provides fine fishing and scuba diving.

Open Bay, indenting the bottom of the "H", and a small bight north of Nelson Bay, at its top, give anchorage to boaters escaping the summertime bustle of

Garrison Bay and Mosquito Pass from Youngs Hill

Roche Harbor. Do not go ashore, for the entire island is privately owned. Approximately 80 acres at Kellett Bluff on the tip of the southwest lobe of the island is a lighthouse reservation; however, the steepness of the shore makes landing there impractical.

One mile due north of Henry Island, chunky Battleship Island, with "smokestacks" of three trees, surely does resemble its namesake in both size and shape. Battleship, along with Barren Island (lying to the east of the entrance to Roche Harbor near Davidson Head) and Pole Island (in the north entrance of Mosquito Pass), are all part of the San Juan Islands Wilderness Area.

SAN JUAN COUNTY PARK

Park Area: 12 acres
Access: Ferry to San Juan Island or boat
Facilities: Campsites, fireplaces, water, restrooms, picnic tables, groceries, boat launching. Camping fee, reservations for groups of eight or more
Attractions: Boating, scuba diving, snorkeling, beachcombing

The story is told that long ago a number of Indians stricken with smallpox plunged into icy San Juan waters to rid themselves of their burning fever; as a result they subsequently died of pneumonia. The tiny bay on the west side of San

San Juan Island County Park

Juan Island where the tragedy occurred has since that time been called Smallpox Bay.

Despite its unfortunate history, today the bay is of more pleasant significance, for it is the site of popular San Juan County Park. Located on the West Side Road, 3½ miles (5¼ km) south of the Beaverton Valley Road intersection, the park occupies the land at the head of the bay and an abandoned orchard on a bluff.

Although the park "officially" has only 18 campsites, up to 400 people have been crammed into the 12 acres on summer weekends. Miraculously the park survives the pressure of such numbers, but obviously there has to be a limit. To better enjoy the area, visit off season.

In winter, when it is uncrowded, it is a relaxing spot with exquisite nighttime views across Haro Strait to the lights of Vancouver Island. Explore the shores of the bay, or saunter through twisted madronas to the top of the bluff, but even the healthy would risk pneumonia by attempting to swim in the bay.

With divespots within walking distance of campsites, the park is a favorite among scuba divers. Easy snorkeling is found in the bay, while the rocky bottom which drops off steeply just offshre is a challenge to more experienced divers.

Gulls, and sometimes seals, congregate on Low Island, 100 yards offshore—another of the bird refuges of the San Juan Islands Wilderness.

The tiny log cabin in the campground was built at the turn of the century as a home for a widower homesteader and his daughter. While the building was under construction, the pair lived in a cave which he dug in the side of a nearby hill. The cabin once had an outside stairway to provide access to the daughter's bedroom on the second floor.

122

LIME KILN LIGHTHOUSE

Just past San Juan County Park, West Side Road turns from blacktop to gravel and continues southward through sparse timber. In 3 miles (4¾ km) it curves around a hill and burst suddenly into open marine views. To the right, at the bend of the hairpin curve a single lane dirt road leads to Lime Kiln Lighthouse. The road may be driven, but it is narrow with little turn-around space. Park at the roadhead instead, being careful to not block either road. Walk the gravel road or scramble along the rocky shoreline to the lighthouse. Loop hike is about ¾ mile (1 km).

Deadman Bay, just below the road intersection, is a popular scuba diving spot. It was named for a sensational murder which occurred here in the late 1800s. Land surrounding the bay is private property.

Built in 1919, the lighthouse, now automated, has been in continuous operation since that time. The State Parks Commission recently took over maintenance of the surrounding property for public use. At this site was one of the earliest lime kiln operations in the San Juans; excavations and remnants of some of the old structures can still be seen.

Hand carried boats can be launched at the cove on the north side of the park. Attempts to build a dock there have been thwarted by the heavy waves of winter storms.

South of Lime Kiln Lighthouse the 2-mile stretch of West Side Road is one of the most spectacular in the islands, well worth the drive in itself. Twisting high on rocky bluffs, it offers views outward across the glittering expanse of Haro Strait and steeply downward to waves beating against the rugged toes of San Juan Island. In spring masses of California poppies flame between rocky outcrops.

FALSE BAY

More than 200 acres of strange creatures to investigate—skittery purple shore crabs, two-foot, flame-colored ribbon worms, shoe-shaped chitons, prehistoric-appearing clingfish, barnacles and rock oysters (jingle shells) fated to spend life fastened to but one rock, with never a change of scenery.

Lime Kiln Lighthouse

False Bay at low tide

Shallow, nearly-circular False Bay is located on the southern end of San Juan Island, with its narrow mouth opening onto Haro Strait. The shores provide a pleasant beach walk at moderate-to-high tides, but the real fun comes at low water when the entire bay nearly dries. Don rubber boots and wander through the muck to observe seashore life.

To reach False Bay from Friday Harbor drive west out of town on Spring Street. At an intersection 1½ miles from town turn left (south) onto False Bay Road, which can be followed for 3½ more miles to the bay.

The bay is owned and carefully monitored as a biological study area for the University of Washington. Several scientific theses have been written on the ecological systems found here. The contained environment, sheltered as it is from the disturbing action of large waves, allows the study of discrete marine populations. Look all you wish, but **do not kill or collect any specimens.** Walk carefully to avoid damaging any of the marine life.

A good seashore guide such as **Seashore Life of Puget Sound, the Strait of Georgia and the San Juan Archipelago,** by Eugene Kozloff, or **Living Shores of the Pacific Northwest** by Lynnwood S. Smith, helps immeasurably in the identification and understanding of these invertebrates. A magnifying glass is also useful. A clear glass jar filled with fresh sea water aids in studying delicate animals; slip the specimen carefully into the jar to observe it, then quickly return it to its home. If the water becomes too warm it may die. Handle shell-less creatures with damp hands to avoid damaging their protective slime coating.

When walking this, or any beach, avoid dislocating stones which harbor marine life. Certain marine specimens live only on the exposed tops of rocks, while others seek the protection of the bottom; eggs are often attached to the undersides of beach rocks. If a stone is lifted and then replaced upside down, the invertebrates formerly on top will suffocate on the bottom, while the others die of exposure on top.

Study a single rock to see the many kinds of life it supports. Pick up a piece of seaweed and check it out for "hitchhikers". Pools hold tiny fish waiting to be released by the next incoming tide.

Overnight camping or beach fires are not permitted at False Bay.

SAN JUAN NATIONAL HISTORICAL PARK

Perhaps it was a kindly hand of Fate that determined that the United States and England be brought to the brink of war over a pig. With tempers as testy as they were, the deceased party could easily have been a man instead of a recalcitrant porker. As it was, the military authorities felt foolish being at loggerheads over the honor of a pig, permitting more rational minds to prevail and avert a serious war.

The Treaty of 1846 caused it all. When British and American negotiators signed the document establishing the Oregon Territory boundary, they chose to overlook the vague language defining the boundary through a cluster of "worthless" islands lying between the mainland and Vancouver Island. Hudson's Bay Company, however, was well aware of the value of the timber, fur, fish and grazing lands of the San Juan Islands. They claimed the territory for Queen Victoria by establishing an outpost overlooking the Strait of Juan de Fuca on the southern end of "Bellevue" Island, as San Juan Island was then called. Meanwhile, the American westward expansion brought to this paradise Yankee settlers who scraped out homesteads, disregarding the property claims and, perhaps more important, the tax collectors of the British.

Lyman Cutlar chose as his farmsite a few acres in the middle of a Hudson's Bay sheep pasture. There he built a shack and planted potatoes. Cutlar was mighty attached to his crop, for that spring of 1859 he had rowed 40 miles round trip across the Strait of Juan de Fuca to purchase the seed potatoes. Thus, when a Hudson's Bay pig proceeded to willfully and regularly trespass into his potato patch, he violently objected. After registering a complaint with the unsympathetic Hudson's Bay agent, Cutlar solved the problem by dispatching the offending pig with his rifle.

Tempers flared and Cutlar was threatened with arrest. In somewhat pithy language he questioned the jurisdiction of the Crown, and appealed to American authorities. James Douglas, Governor of British Columbia, who had long been

Sign on interpretive trail at American Camp, San Juan National Historical Park

rankled by the incursions of American settlers, saw an opportunity to settle the matter of British sovereignty in the islands, and ordered a ship to San Juan Island to support the Hudson's Bay position.

American and English militarists who scouted the waters in the years following the Treaty of 1846 had noted that San Juan Island strategically guarded the Strait of Juan de Fuca, Haro Strait and the mouth of the Fraser River. They were determined the territory should not fall into the hands of a potential foe. Soon both sides were massing ships, men and armaments. At times they were only a bullet away from all-out war. The superior British flotilla could have easily leveled American fortifications with their heavy guns. However, if battle had really begun all American settlers in the area would enter into the fracas and the British would be outnumbered. Moreover, the fight was sure to spread to Vancouver Island where there were nearly four American "foreigners" to every British subject. Leaders on both sides realized that any serious war would bathe the islands in the blood of hundreds of American and British citizens.

Lt. General Winfield Scott was dispatched by President James Buchanan to take command of American matters in the San Juan archipelago. Arriving in October of 1859, and finding that battle had fortunately not yet begun, he proposed to Douglas that the island be jointly occupied by equal forces of the two factions until arbitration could settle the boundary dispute. The British eventually accepted this plan, and American Camp was established on the southern tip of the island on barren slopes near the Hudson's Bay trading post. Meanwhile the British marines landed on the shores of a protected harbor on the northwest side of the island, which they named Garrison Bay.

Once the threat of all-out war in the San Juans was assuaged, the U.S. government turned its attention to more urgent internal problems in the southern states. With the beginning of the Civil War in April of 1861, the San Juan dispute was relegated to a diplomatic back burner. England, too, was embroiled in domestic problems and did not press for settlement of the dispute. Time wore on and the hastily erected tents at English and American Camps were replaced by permanent barracks, hospitals and social halls. Timber was cleared for parade grounds and gardens. Duty was good on San Juan Island.

Finally, with the boundary commission at an impasse, the question was submitted to an impartial arbitrator, Kaiser Wilhelm I of Germany, who in October of 1872, decided in favor of the United States. The dispute was finally settled . . . thirteen years after an English boar filled his jowls with American potatoes and thus stepped into history.

Several excellent books on the complete history of the war are available. Keith Murray's **The Pig War** and **The San Juan Water Boundary Question** by James McCabe are both quite authoritative.

Following withdrawal of armed forces, the lands of American and English Camp were privately owned. In 1966 Congress commemorated the peaceful settlement of the dispute by designating the two areas as San Juan National Historical Park and parcels of land on Griffin and Garrison Bays were purchased. Today some interpretive and recreational facilities have been completed and more are planned. Archeological digs completed by park personnel in 1977 searched for Indian and pioneer artifacts.

The park grounds are open during daylight hours year around, although the buildings at English Camp are closed offseason. Information is also available at park headquarters at American Camp.

Split rail fence at American Camp

ENGLISH CAMP

Park Area: 529 acres
Access: Ferry to San Juan Island or boat
Facilities: Dock, picnic tables, pit toilets, *no overnight camping, no water*
Attractions: Historical display, hiking, boating, clams.

The most interesting of the Pig War relics are found at English Camp. Three of the original buildings have been restored and one houses artifacts and an interpretive display. Park rangers wearing dashing replicas of English and American military uniforms present historical programs during summer weekends.

To reach English Camp from Friday Harbor, follow the Roche Harbor Road which curves around the north end of the Island. At a major intersection, 8½ miles (13½ km) from Friday Harbor turn left (south) from Roche Harbor Road onto Beaverton Valley Road. Entrance to English Camp is on the right in 1½ miles (2½ km).

From the parking area a 200 yard path, edged by a picturesque split rail fence, leads to the military site on Garrison Bay. The blockhouse near the beach was built to protect the marines from marauding Indians, rather than from warring Yankees, and also served as a guard house. A traditional formal garden, fenced against deer and rabbits, is typical of those planted during the time. Near the barracks grows a spreading big leaf maple tree; at one time it was the largest of its kind in the world, but now is slightly outranked by one in Oregon.

Remnants of one of the old docks is still visible near the blockhouse. A small dock with space for a few dinghys is now located farther north along the beach. The 1½-mile boat excursion from Roche Harbor to English Camp winds through lovely Mosquito Pass and the narrow entrance to Westcott Bay. Consult a good chart for the location of numerous shoals along the way; Garrison Bay is quite shallow throughout and deep keeled vessels should enter with care.

In summer the bay is often filled with boats anchored and rafted together. Skippers may also anchor at Westcott Bay, then dinghy to Bell Point and walk the trail to English Camp.

BELL POINT

A level, ½-mile hike through madrona and fir to pretty Bell Cove on Westcott Bay, where rusted spikes and planks still scarring old trees give evidence of pioneer use of the area. The signed trail starts on the north side of the English Camp clearing near the shore.

The beaches of Bell Point may be closed during certain seasons, although Bell Cove is normally open year around. Observe posted signs. Dig clams only if you intend to use them, and observe limits; heavy public use of the clam beds could exhaust them in the near future. Tides permitting, the beach may also be walked to Bell Cove.

For an alternative return to English Camp, follow the old wagon track which heads east from Bell Point, skirting Westcott Bay. In about ¼ mile the route reaches a clearing. Turn right (south), following the grassy track between the old-growth timber of Bell Point and a thick stand of recent-growth firs. Listen here for the distinctive trilling song of the chipping sparrow which nests in the

English Camp

area. The track eventually emerges at the north corner of the English Camp clearing. Total distance of the loop hike is about 1 mile (1½ km).

GUSS ISLAND

Wooded Guss Island, named for a San Juan storekeeper during British occupation, is also part of the park. Located only 300 yards offshore, it can easily be reached by canoe or kayak. Clam digging is not permitted on the posted beaches of Guss Island or English Camp at any time. Clams have been seriously depleted here and the beaches have been closed to allow them to reestablish.

BRITISH MILITARY CEMETERY

A small plot on the slopes of Young Hill holds the graves of seven marines who died during the British occupation of San Juan Island. Find the trailhead to the cemetery at the picnic area which is next to the parking lot at English Camp. The signed trail begins at the edge of the meadow and wends steadily uphill along an old overgrown wagon track.

Sun filters through second growth alder, fir and madrona. Walk quietly and perhaps be rewarded with glimpses of black-tailed deer, or occasionally great horned owls, blinking sleepily in the trees. An owl's favorite perching spot can sometimes be located by watching for piles of droppings beneath the tree. These owls take large numbers of rodents, and are responsible, even more than eagles and hawks, for controlling the island's rabbit population. The winter wren nests here—listen for its lovely sustained warbling song as you hike.

Although the route crosses the Beaverton Valley Road in ¼ mile, hikers must begin the trip at the parking lot, as there is no parking space along the road. Above the highway the trail continues, lined by a split rail fence.

The cemetery, in a grassy clearing, is reached in another ¼ mile. A neat white picket fence encloses four tombstones of service men who all died accidently while serving at English Camp. The stones tell the story of each mishap; note that one commemorates two marines who were drowned at sea. Two other graves are unmarked.

Total distance from the parking lot is less than ½ mile (¾ km), elevation gain 250 feet (75 meters).

Several of the trees in the clearing were killed or badly scarred by a 1972 fire. Take heed of the havoc that a cigarette ash accidently dropped in dry grass can cause.

YOUNG HILL

Probably the most spectacular viewpoint on San Juan Island. The trail is steep, but well worth the effort on a clear day. From the cemetery the beaten path can be seen going straight uphill over open rocky slopes to the top of the mountain. Scramble up to the 650-foot (200 meter) summit where British

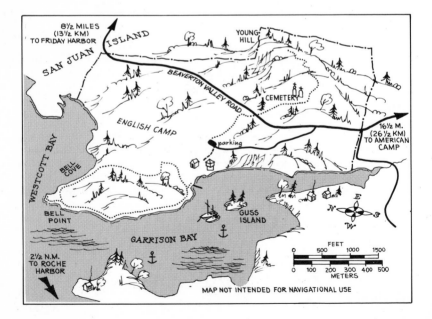

MAP NOT INTENDED FOR NAVIGATIONAL USE

Historical display at English Camp

marines maintained an observation post during the Pig War. Elevation gain from cemetery, 320 feet (97½ meters) in less than ¼ mile (⅓ km).

Views, views, views. Henry Island, White and Bazelgette Points, Mosquito Pass and Westcott and Garrison Bays merge in a mosaic of land and water. Mitchell Bay, whose entrance is obscured by land, looks like a small lake. Southward can be seen the snowy peaks of the Olympic Mountains, while to the north are the Canadian Gulf Islands, marked by the imposing profile of Saltspring Island. Across Haro Strait lies Vancouver Island where, over 100 years ago, British frigates sailed forth to uphold the sovereignty of the crown.

Stroll to the east side of the hill for views of Mt. Baker. Looking southeast from the summit, immediately above the silhouette of Mt. Erie on Fidalgo Island, on a very clear day Sloan Peak can be seen; ranging southward are the misty outlines of Mt. Baring, Mt. Index and other Stevens Pass peaks, more than 90 miles distant.

Early morning at Garrison Bay

AMERICAN CAMP

Park Area: 1,222 acres
Access: Ferry to San Juan Island or boat
Facilities: Picnic tables, pit toilets, *no water, no overnight camping,* fires on
 beach only (by permit)
Attractions: Historical display, hiking, boating, beachcombing

Not as much visible history as at English Camp, but a marine panorama, sylvan hikes and miles of surf-swept beach. To reach American Camp from English Camp, continue south on Beaverton Valley Road and in 1½ miles (2¼ km) turn right (west) onto Griffin Bay Road. Follow the road as it meanders north, then west, and finally south and becomes West Side Road as it heads down-island. The road bends eastward 9 miles (14½ km) from English Camp, and is signed as Bailer Hill Road. Turn right (south) in 3 (4¾ km) more miles onto False Bay Road, which skirts the bay and finally intersects with Cattle Point Road, 15½ miles (24¾ km) total distance from English Camp. Turn right; park entrance in 1 more mile (1½ km).

To travel directly to American Camp from Friday Harbor, at the Y intersection on the south side of town, bear left (south) on Argyle Avenue. Follow the arterial south and then west to its intersection with Cattle Point Road. The route is well signed. Total distance to park, 5 miles (8 km).

For visitors arriving by boat, there are no docking facilities at American Camp; however, small boats may be beached on gentle shores on either side of the park. Griffin Bay provides the only semi-protected anchorages; when entering the bay carefully check nautical charts and depthfinders for the location of numerous submerged rocks. The north beach of the park is about 6½ nautical miles from either Friday Harbor or Fisherman Bay.

INTERPRETIVE TRAIL

Just inside the park boundary a right hand fork of the road leads to the park headquarters and information center. Just to the east, is a picnic area, shaded by old fruit trees, and the starting point for a ¾-mile (1 km) self-guided interpretive trail. Signs at numerous points along the walk narrate Pig War history and interesting features of the park. At the top of the ridge, Pickett's Redoubt commands views of American Camp and surrounding waters stretching to Victoria. Still in evidence are the earthworks (redoubt) thrown up by American troops, where five cannons were mounted.

PARK HISTORY PROGRAMS

On summer weekends and holidays the national park presents an outstanding series of programs and special events, at American and English Camps, which attract both tourists and local residents. The programs are designed to make history come alive—in some, park personnel wearing period costumes recreate the daily lives of soldiers, laundresses and settlers during the time of the Pig

Pickett's Redoubt at American Camp

Evening folkdancing at English Camp

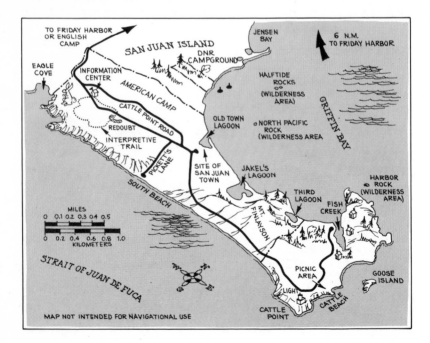

War. Authentic props such as a Sibley tent and laundry tubs fashioned from whiskey barrels complete the scene. For other programs employees and visitors take part in song fests, square dances and games reminiscent of the 1860s.

Excellent evening fireside talks, slide shows and movies on the history, flora and fauna and natural features of the region are also regularly presented.

RABBITS

This long arm of San Juan Island is largely covered by soft glacial till deposited by retreating ice centuries ago. The loose mixture of sand, stone and boulders, ideal for tunnelling has made American Camp a "Watership Down West" for San Juan rabbits. Their evidence is everywhere—droppings cover the ground to the extent that in many places more dung than dirt is visible.

Tunnel entrances make the grounds look like a bombed battlefield. At one spot along the interpretive trail the soft soil has been dug out in order to reveal the network of tunnels comprising a warren.

Plump bunnies can be seen everywhere at almost any time of day. Hunting or trapping has not been permitted since the park was established in 1966, and with such favorable conditions they have multiplied—and multiplied—and multiplied!

The rabbits are a major food source for eagles, great horned owls and other predatory birds that live on the island. While the rabbit population fluctuates somewhat, a fairly stable natural balance has been established between the predators and their food supply.

Rabbit tunnels at American Camp

SOUTH SHORE WALK

Leave the interpretive trail and wander open slopes above the water to enjoy the austere beauty of the park. No formal trails. In late summer the inland section of the slope is covered with patches of nettles and Canadian thistles. Long pants are advised.

Near the edge of the cliff the harsh environment causes the vegetation to be miniaturized. Many species of plants are so tiny that novice botanists can identify them only when they bloom. Collinsias grow less than an inch tall, showing ¼-inch purple blossoms in late May. Lupin, whose distinctive hand-shaped leaves grow over 4 inches across on the alpine slopes of Mt. Rainier, here have ground-hugging leaves smaller than a thumbnail.

Bays along this section of the island are unlike those found anywhere else in the San Juans. The soft glacial till, scooped out by winds from the Strait of Juan de Fuca, form perfect, grassy amphitheaters dropping steeply to beaches jammed with huge driftwood logs. Explore the small coves if you wish, but first consider the stiff, 50-foot scramble back up to the top.

The rounded bay to the west was the site of the original Hudson's Bay Company settlement. Artifacts can sometimes be found in the vicinity—rabbits dig them out occasionally and toss them aside, with total disregard for their historical significance. Unauthorized digging for artifacts (by humans) is prohibited, and any that are found on the surface must be turned over to the park ranger.

If hiking legs need further exercise, traverse the bank eastward, staying well above the shore. The earth is soft on the high bank near the edge, and footing may be insecure. When the slope gentles, drop down to South Beach near the parking lot. Return to the information center via the road. Total distance of loop hike about 3 miles (4¾ km).

SOUTH BEACH

For road access to 2 miles of unbroken beach edging the Strait of Juan de Fuca, turn right off American Camp Road onto Pickett's Lane. It is ½ mile to the parking lot. Lightweight boats may be carried the short distance from the parking area for launching, surf permitting.

Use great care in small boats here and on Griffin Bay. The wind and current can be extremely strong and attempting to maneuver an underpowered boat under such conditions can be a frightening experience.

When storms kick up in the straits, wave action on the beach is very heavy. Exciting to watch, but drift logs are dangerous at these times; stay well away from moving logs.

With calm weather and favorable tides the beach can be walked all the way east to Cattle Point, 2 miles from the parking lot. Very little marine life is found on the gravel beach. Constant movement of the surf-tumbled rock lets nothing survive for long.

Picnicking is permitted, but fires must be built near the water, far enough away from driftwood to prevent spreading. Fire permits must be obtained from the ranger on duty. Motorized vehicles are not allowed in any off-road area.

F. SAN JUAN ISLAND

SAN JUAN TOWN

When American troops built their stronghold on San Juan Island, a shanty town sprang up nearby just outside the military camp boundary on the shore of Griffin Bay. Shopkeepers in San Juan Town sold a few supplies to the soldiers, settlers and Indians, but it was soon apparent that liquor was the commodity in greatest demand. Other enterprising merchants brought in Indian women for "nefarious purposes". Robberies, assaults and sometimes murders took place, with open defiance of civil and military officers. Authorities were able to tame the town a bit, however it always remained a center for booze, brothels and brawls.

In 1873, when San Juan County was established, the new commissioners felt that San Juan Town, with its rowdy reputation, was unsuitable for a county seat. Instead they selected a few acres at Friday Harbor on the north end of the island. In time businesses drifted away from Old San Juan Town (especially when Friday Harbor also acquired a saloon), and by the late 1800s the once-thriving village was a ghost town. The deserted buildings were accidentally burned to the ground in 1890, bringing to a close the career of the colorful, if somewhat tarnished, village.

The saltwater lagoon visible on the north side of American Camp Road is just west of the old townsite. A few footings of the original buildings have been excavated and can be found by searching the grassy fields. Halfway down the hill the track of an old road is still visible. Removal of any artifact found here, or elsewhere in the park is illegal—such articles must be turned over to a park ranger.

GRIFFIN BAY

Early sailing ships hove to in Griffin Bay waiting out westerlies whipping the Strait of Juan de Fuca. Today fast moving power boats whiz by in San Juan Channel, rarely stopping to enjoy the languid pleasures of the bay.

The gentle shore extends ½ mile northwest from the San Juan Town lagoon to the park boundary; driftwood and some interesting marine life. Visitors who wrestle portable boats downhill from the road to the beach will be rewarded with a leisurely paddle the length of the park.

Although the beach slopes gradually, a number of rocks are scattered at or near the water's surface. Barren Half Tide Rocks and North Pacific Rock can be seen just offshore, while Harbor Rock lies farther east off the tip of Cape San Juan. Nesting grounds for marine birds, these three groups of rocks are part of the San Juan Islands Wilderness.

EUROPEAN SKYLARK

The vicinity of American Camp is the only known nesting area in the continental U.S. of the European skylark, although they have also been recently sighted on Whidbey Island and the Olympic Peninsula. Introduced to Vancouver Island by the English, who brought several pairs from Europe, the birds winged their way to San Juan Island where they have also taken up residence.

Skylarks frequent open grassy fields where they forage for seeds and insects and build their nests. Its drab brown-streaked plumage appears similar to that of

Twinflower (left) and calypso (right), found near Jakel's Lagoon. Calypsos are an endangered flower species

a female house sparrow, however it can be distinguished from the sparrow by its slightly larger size (7-7½") and its distinctly marked white stomach, wingtips and outer tail feathers.

The European skylark's popularity arises from its melodious song in flight—a high-pitched, sustained torrent of runs and trills as it hovers 200 feet in the air. Listen for it as you roam the park.

JAKEL'S LAGOON

While American Camp is impressive, it can at times seem bleak. Jakel's Lagoon, a secluded nook of the park, offers a pleasing contrast, with ferns, rich moss carpet and tall firs. At the urging of the Nature Conservancy the road has been closed to vehicles to protect the eagles' nesting areas and the delicate ecology of the lagoon.

The lagoon itself has been set aside as a natural environmental study area. It is used by the Friday Harbor Laboratories as a collecting site for marine specimens and has been the subject of several studies and PhD theses.

The trailhead to the lagoon is located a few hundred feet east of the Pickett's Lane intersection on American Camp Road, where a side road branches north, ending at a gate in a short distance. All vehicles are prohibited beyond this point. There is parking space for a few cars; use care not to block the gate in case of an emergency.

Hike the abandoned road downhill, dipping into the forest. A confusing network of old roads criss-crosses the hillside; keep bearing downhill and eastward, staying on the main road, avoiding side trails. When the only four-way

intersection is reached, turn left—the lagoon is about 200 feet (65 meters) farther.

Signs posted along the trail warn hikers not to smoke while on the trail. Camp fires are also forbidden in the forest and on the beaches. In the dry summer the fire hazard here is extreme and a spark could start a blaze which would destroy the entire wooded area, bringing death to the birds and animals that live there. There are no garbage cans; pack out all litter.

A grassy point protruding into the southwest side of the lagoon is a fit spot for a Hobbitt home. In winter when the forest drips with San Juan mist, and fog lies heavily over the lagoon, one can easily imagine magical creatures scurrying in the undergrowth.

With moderate-to-low tides the Griffin Bay beach can be walked between the site of San Juan Town and the lagoon for a loop trip and an opportunity to beachcomb. Round trip is 1¼ miles (2 km).

THIRD LAGOON

Another, smaller lagoon lies ½ mile farther east. Old Town Lagoon is the first, Jakel's is the second and this, appropriately, is simply known as Third Lagoon. It may be reached one of several ways: the easiest route, tide permitting, is to walk the gravel beach east from Jakel's Lagoon.

A second route leaves the east end of Jakel's Lagoon and heads uphill, then traverses the edge of a steep bluff, 25 feet above the water. Not an easy route, in fact darned slippery during wet weather, but the beauty of the forest makes it worthwhile. In spring find calypso, twinflower and bleeding heart popping through the carpet of rich moss. Some short sections of brushbeating may be necessary, but for the most part animal trails or an abandoned foot trail can be followed. Stay within sight of the water except when brush must be detoured.

For a third route, return to the abandoned road from Jakel's Lagoon and continue east. The road climbs to the top of a ridge, then descends again; where

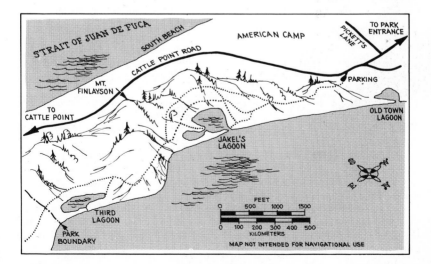

Beach near Third Lagoon

Cattle Point

it levels off at the bottom, watch for a faint road on the left which leads to the lagoon. If the side road is missed, continue until the lagoon is clearly in sight through open timber and head cross country.

Just beyond the lagoon the road is gated at the eastern park boundary; from here it crosses private property to Fish Creek. Round trip from the parking lot is about 2½ miles (4 km). Elevation gain (on return), 130 feet (45 meters).

MT. FINLAYSON

The rolling hill of Mt. Finlayson is the highest point on this end of the island. There are no formal trails, but the wind-swept slopes on the south side may easily be walked to the summit.

Park at the small parking lot above Old Town Lagoon. If space is not available there, cars may be left in the more spacious lot at South Beach, and the hike begun by traversing rolling slopes northeast for ½ mile back to the American Camp Road.

Clamber over the split rail fence and follow the easy route to the 295 foot (90 meter) summit. In some spots a faint wagon track can be followed.

From the mountaintop look north to Griffin Bay and Lopez Island and south across the straits to white Olympic peaks. Ocean freighters ply the straits, bearing cargoes from exotic lands headed for Puget Sound ports. Once they carried silk and tea and spices; today they are laden with plywood and Hondas.

Distance from upper parking lot, 1 mile (1½ km), elevation gain 200 feet (60 meters).

Cattle Point Lighthouse

SAN JUAN CHANNEL

GRIFFIN BAY CAMPGROUND

Area: 19 acres
Access: Boat only
Facilities: Mooring buoys, picnic tables, campsites, fireplaces, pit toilets, water

Facing on Griffin Bay, North of American Camp, a section of forested land with 300 feet of gentle beachfront is a recently developed DNR camp area. Five on-shore campsites with picnic tables and fireplaces are near the beach and farther back in timber. Located only 6 nautical miles from the docks of Friday Harbor, the park is an ideal overnight stop for small boats on voyages of discovery in San Juan Channel.

CATTLE POINT

The white concrete tower of Cattle Point Light has long been a welcome sight to boaters emerging from fog banks of the Strait of Juan de Fuca. Perched on sand dunes 80 feet above the beach, it can be reached by land by a 300-yard trail from the parking lot just south of the National Historical Park, at the "toe" of San Juan Island, or by walking the beach at low tide for 2 miles (3 km) east from South Beach.

The dune area is an ecological rarity in the San Juans. Winds sweeping off the straits pile the sand in great, smooth mounds, which are inviting to walk on and explore. Vehicles of any type are prohibited beyond the parking lot, as the dune area is quite fragile. Farther back from the beach, the sand has been stabilized by tough grass and bramble bushes. Here the ubiquitous San Juan rabbit digs burrows and peers insolently at visitors from the safety of the thicket.

Cattle Beach

CATTLE BEACH PICNIC AREA

Access: Car or boat
Facilities: Picnic tables, pit toilets, *no water*
Attractions: Beachcombing, hiking

Two small gravel and driftwood beaches, separated by a glacier-scoured rock promontory, face on the entrance to San Juan Channel. Beach life is scarce here, but water-smoothed agates are often turned up amid the pebbles.

The Department of Natural Resources picnic area is located ¾ mile (1 km) east of the American Camp boundary, along the Cattle Point Road. Several picnic tables on top of the bluff provide sweeping views of the channel and Lopez Island. Nearby, a concrete building, which was built in 1927 as a Coast Guard radio station, will soon be converted to use as a picnic shelter.

A ¼-mile trail goes south from the picnic area, through timber and along the top of the bluff, to Cattle Point Light. Another steep, and sometimes slippery, trail descends the bank to the small southern bay; the northern bay has a first-class wooden stairway reaching from bluff-top to beach.

Small boats may be landed on either beach, but there is no offshore anchorage. Use great care on this end of the island; tide rips can be quite strong.

GOOSE ISLAND

Just 400 yards off Cattle Beach is Goose Rock, which is owned by the Nature Conservancy and administered by the Friday Harbor Laboratories as a biological preserve. It is one of the few such islands in the San Juans to have nearly natural vegatation.

During pioneer times it was the practice to row sheep to grassy islands for summer grazing. (It was also necessary to frequently row barrels of fresh water to the flocks.) As a result, some plant species were completely wiped out on the islands, and other tougher species took over. For some reason Goose Island escaped this fate, making it a unique botanical study area today.

G. NORTH FROM SPIEDEN CHANNEL

Trending northwest from the busy waterway of Spieden Channel, Spieden and Stuart Islands and their associated smaller islands are similar geologically to the Sucia Islands group to the north. These landfalls are composed of folded, eroded sedimentary beds with long ridges which extend underwater as a network of reefs and shoals which make boat captains wary, but beckon to fishermen and scuba divers. Lying deep in the rain shadow of Vancouver Island, the climate is so dry that the Cactus Islands do, indeed, support cactus.

These are islands to enjoy from the deck of your boat, for aside from the state parks on Stuart Island and the smattering of wildlife refuges, all shore land is privately owned and there are no commercial developments.

SPIEDEN ISLAND

The most striking in appearance of this northwestern group, 480-acre Spieden Island, with its long northern slope neatly forested and its southern side barren except for tawny grass, appears as if a prankish barber had been at work. Lying alongside, to the south, 15-acre Sentinel Island is a miniature duplication of its neighbor.

Reid Harbor

G.   NORTH FROM SPIEDEN CHANNEL

Spieden, which is the only large San Juan island without a bay or harbor of any sort, has not been commercially developed, and until recent years its life has been pleasantly bucolic. In the early 1970s an abortive attempt was made to capitalize on its dry climate and open range land by transforming it into an African game farm and renaming it "Safari Island".

FLATTOP ISLAND AND OTHER BIRD REFUGES

Sentinel Rock, and Center Reef (southeast of Spieden Island), Ripple Island (east of Johns Island), Gull and Shag Reefs (in the Cactus Group), Gull Rock and Flattop Island (northeast of Spieden Island) and White Rock (between Flattop and Waldron Islands) are all part of the San Juan Islands Wilderness.

Although in the past boaters have stopped at Flattop Island, the largest of these bird refuges, public recreational use is now prohibited in order to protect the nesting areas.

Disturbance of nesting birds by humans has a detrimental effect on the survival of the young, for when nests are abandoned, even for a short period of time, the unattended eggs will be broken by predatory birds, or the eggs may chill and fail to hatch.

Nesting gulls are extremely territorial during this time and will viciously defend their foot-square domain against intrusion; if a parent gull is chased from her nest, the frightened chicks often scatter into foreign territory and are killed by rival birds. Boaters must recognize that it is imperative that they stay away from the nesting grounds.

Western grebe and young

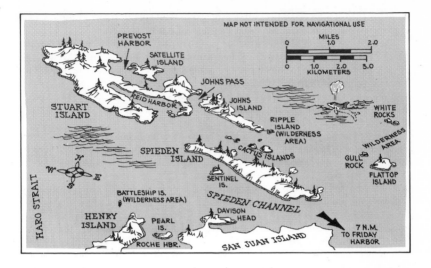

MAP NOT INTENDED FOR NAVIGATIONAL USE

STUART ISLAND

Island Area: 1,786 acres
Park Areas: Reid Harbor—44 acres, Prevost Harbor—40 acres, Turn Point—67.3 acres
Access: Boat only
Facilities (at Reid and Prevost Harbors): Floats, mooring buoys, campsites, picnic tables, stoves, water, pit toilets
Attractions: Clams, crabs, fishing, hiking, sightseeing

Not one, but two marine state parks, back-to-back, spanning a slim neck of land, and a third "walk-to" state park at Turn Point, a former lighthouse reserve.

Stuart Island thrusts deeply toward the Canadian border, only 3 miles from several of the Gulf Islands, making the harbors popular stops for B.C.-bound vacationers. Indeed, the outline of the island itself, ignoring its deep harbors, suggests a boat headed for Canadian waters, and Johns Island as its dinghy in tow.

Reid Harbor and Prevost Marine State Parks, often collectively referred to as Stuart Island State Park, provide fine facilities for overnight boaters. Those who stay awhile longer enjoy the fishing, the beaches and the shellfish, while the more energetic might even sample the forest hikes and pastoral road walks which reveal the serene inner beauty of the island.

Stuart Island lies 3½ nautical miles north northwest of Roche Harbor on San Juan Island. When planning a trip from Roche Harbor to Stuart Island in a small boat consider strong tidal currents and shoal areas in Spieden Channel. The entrance to Reid Harbor is constricted by submerged rocks and shoals. Stay in the middle of the channel or slightly to the west to avoid running aground.

Boats cruising to the north side of the island via Johns Pass should use care at the south entrance to the channel. Kelp marks several rocks and a ½-fathom shoal which extends from the eastern tip of the island. Give all obstructions a wide berth; a strong flood tide sets eastward here at speeds up to 5 knots. Check a good navigational chart for exact position of hazards.

The ½-mile recess of Reid Harbor is one of the best anchorages in the San Juans. The enclosing arms of the island drop off sharply to 5 fathoms, giving good anchorages almost up to the shoreline, while the gravel beach at the head of the bay is gradual enough for small craft to land easily.

A dock and float on the north shore, two floats anchored near the head of the bay, and fifteen mooring buoys spaced about the harbor provide easy tie-ups for about forty boats.

Prevost Harbor, on the north side, with its broader beaches, offers a different perspective of the island. The only safe entrance to the harbor is by Charles Point, west of Satellite Island; do not attempt the channel on the east as it is dangerously rocky and shallow.

The state park contains a dock, with float, centered on a bight, seven buoys and several good anchorages, although there may be some difficulty getting hooks to dig through the thick eelgrass at the bottom of the harbor.

Boats opting to anchor in a superb little bay on the north side of the harbor at Satellite Island should be wary of a large rock, submerged at tides above 8 feet, which lies near the center of the entrance. Satellite Island is owned by the YMCA, which maintains a summer camp there, and does not encourage visitors.

Tucked behind the protective wing of Charles Point lie a county dock and a few homes. No facilities or provisions are available here.

Stuart Island has a population of less than thirty permanent residents, living in homes scattered about the island. A small private airfield on the northwest tip of the island serves occupants of summer homes there. Fishing and farming have provided a livelihood for islanders since the days of early homesteading. The reef

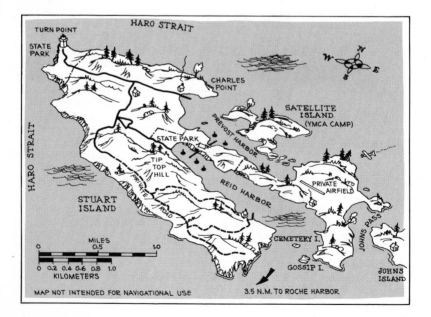

Clamming at Reid Harbor

netting site off the mouth of Reid Harbor has been fished continuously by Indians and their descendents for six generations.

The shores do not exhibit the sculptured sandstone cliffs so characteristic of the northern Sucia Islands group—instead the steep banks are heavily covered with vegetation almost down to the water line. The rounded, forested dome of TipTop Hill, the highest point on the island, rises 640 feet (195 meters) above Reid Harbor.

REID AND PREVOST HARBOR STATE PARKS

Situated on the high bank above Prevost Harbor and on either side of the marsh at the head of Reid Harbor are nineteen state park campsites with fireplaces, all pleasantly shaded by light timber. Water faucets are conveniently located throughout the campgrounds.

The beaches of Prevost Harbor make for interesting low tide exploration. Walk carefully to avoid crushing Dungeness and rock crabs which burrow in the beach seaweed. Gentle probing of the grass may yield some of dinner table size, but remember that any crabs left stranded in the sun may dry out and die. Undersized crabs should be returned to a protected, damp spot or put into the water.

Most tidelands outside the park are privately owned and posted. The park's gravel beaches, especially the one at the head of Reid Harbor, provide first-rate clamming for littlenecks and some butter clams. Those with the stamina to dig deep enough may claim some geoducks.

A ½-mile trail connects the Prevost Harbor dock with the head of Reid Harbor. Catch the cross-island trail south from the dock, following it past the side trail to the toilets. Just before dropping down to the Reid Harbor dock, a trail branches right (west) along the top of the ridge. Pretty views through frames

Stuart Island cemetery. Plastic flowers discourage nibbling by deer

of twisted, red-barked madronas down to sleek boats bobbing at their moorings in Reid Harbor.

In about ½ mile the trail turns sharply downhill for a short but extremely steep section (slippery when wet). At the bottom, in a marshy flat, bear left at a trail fork and head east for 300 yards, emerging at the campground at the northwest corner of Reid Harbor.

CEMETERY AND GOSSIP ISLANDS

Lying on the east side of the Reid Harbor entrance are two undeveloped marine state park islands. The larger of the two, Gossip Island (also sometimes known as George Island), is about an acre of rock and grass and a few scruffy trees; at low tide it nearly joins the Stuart mainland. Smaller Cemetery Island, lying slightly farther into the harbor, is nearly barren.

Dinghy adventurers can paddle or putt out from their anchorages to walk the beaches, to watch the boating traffic and perhaps wave at an incoming friend, or just to have an entire island to themselves for a day. Fires or overnight camping are not permitted.

The water surrounding the two islands is designated as an Underwater Marine Recreation Area for use by skin divers.

STUART ISLAND SCHOOL AND CEMETERY

An easy stretch of the legs gives visitors an opportunity to gain insight into the history and lives of the people who make this island their home.

Find the trail which skirts the southern boundary of Reid Harbor State Park in the campground at the head of the bay. The route, along the county road, climbs

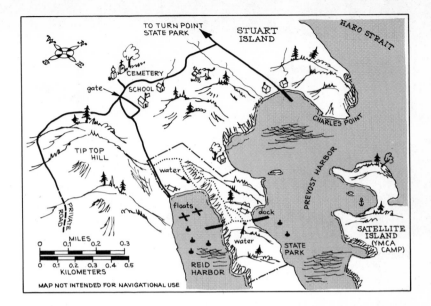

TO TURN POINT STATE PARK

STUART ISLAND

HARO STRAIT

CEMETERY

gate

SCHOOL

CHARLES POINT

TIP TOP HILL

water

PREVOST HARBOR

floats

PRIVATE ROAD

dock

SATELLITE ISLAND (YMCA CAMP)

MILES
0   0.1   0.2   0.3

water

STATE PARK

0   0.1   0.2   0.3   0.4   0.5
KILOMETERS

REID HARBOR

MAP NOT INTENDED FOR NAVIGATIONAL USE

gradually uphill. In about ½ mile watch for a fork on the right which leads to the tiny school in a clearing.

The classic, one-room schoolhouse has served several generations of children who lived on Stuart, Johns and Spieden Islands. In early days the children from the other islands would row to Stuart daily, in all weather, and then hike overland to school. Later, outboard motors made the trip easier, but still somewhat hazardous at times.

One December day in 1961, while all of the school's youngsters were on a boat outing, the boat sank and all aboard were drowned. The school remained closed for 16 years following the tragedy, and local children commuted to San Juan Island. In the fall of 1977 it reopened with an enrollment of eight.

To find the historic little cemetery, continue west on the path past the school to its junction with a dirt road. Turn right, down the road, and in a few yards watch on the left for a faint track leading to the cemetery.

Spanning almost a century of island time, the gravestones tell the story of many settlers who lived here for long years, and others who enjoyed this lovely, though sometimes harsh land for only a brief while.

Examine the gravestones, speculate about the lives of these people, but remember to treat the cemetery with respect.

Round trip from Reid Harbor to the cemetery about 1½ miles (2½ km).

TURN POINT STATE PARK

Far on the western tip of Stuart Island, a lighthouse blinks warning to freighters, fishermen and pleasure boats traveling the waters of Haro Strait. Turn Point Light, so named because it marks the point where boats must turn in the channel, was established at the beginning of the century on a tract of land high atop a rocky cape, with a sweeping 300°-view of the surrounding sea.

Prevost Harbor

Originally the point was the home of Indians who fished the nearby waters. Later, after the construction of the lighthouse, a succession of lighthouse keepers lived here, raised their families and oftentimes left their names imprinted on the history of the area. In recent years the lighthouse has become automated; it seems unfortunate, at times, that fine old traditions must give way to modern technology. Today the 67 acres of land are leased by the Washington State Parks and Recreation Commission as an undeveloped state park.

Turn Point is best reached by an overland hike from Reid Harbor. The steep cliffs below the point and the treacherous water offshore make landing by boat impractical. Catch the trail described above, beginning at the southwest corner of Reid Harbor. The schoolhouse may be bypassed by staying on the main trail until it joins the road. Follow the dirt road north through a gate and past several farmhouses.

Walking the quiet, tree-shaded road is like stepping into time suspended. The nautical bustle of the harbors seems a planet away. Rarely is anyone seen along the deserted track. Even if some farmhouses appear unoccupied, all land is private property. Do not trespass.

In about 1½ miles the route intersects with the Prevost road. Several homes can be seen down the road on the right, beyond it Satellite Island and on a clear day, Mt. Baker hovering above. Turn left at the intersection and continue past rolling fields where cattle share pasturage with deer. At about 2½ miles (4 km) Turn Point State Park is reached.

Views in all directions across Haro Strait to Canadian Islands and down the 50-foot cliff to the sea churning against the flanks of the point. Walk with care as footing at the edge of the cliff can be insecure.

Take the hike in the late afternoon to enjoy the fiery sunset behind Vancouver Island and the crimson afterglow, but pack along a flashlight for the return trip through the forest. Fires and overnight camping are not permitted at Turn Point. Round trip from Reid Harbor about 5 miles (8 km).

H. ORCAS ISLAND

Orcas Island is unique among the San Juans, with its two long sounds thrusting deep into the interior of the land, giving it more shoreline and more protected waters than any of its neighboring islands. In addition, it has taller mountains and more surface area than any of the others, although it only exceeds San Juan Island by a mere 1½ square miles.

Proud residents can certainly boast that it has more of everything, including the largest park, Moran State Park; however with all this bounty, Orcas Island has only limited saltwater lands open to public use.

This may soon be remedied, for as of 1979 a movement was underway to establish a beach-front park at Crescent Beach, east of Eastsound. At the same time a second park has also been proposed at Fishing Bay, immediately in front of the town. If either, or both, of these parks should come into being, they will make fine additions to the public recreational facilities on the island.

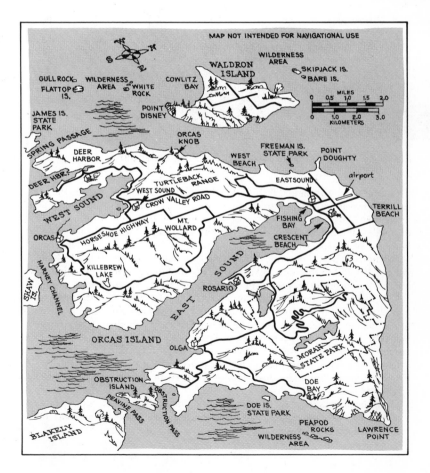

H. ORCAS ISLAND

Entrance Mountain from Moran State Park viewpoint

Orcas Island was named in 1792 for the viceroy of Mexico, not for the whale that was so abundant in surrounding waters. It is doubtful that those early Spanish explorers deliberately chose the name for its double meaning, for they normally named major landfalls such as this after important political or religious figures, not for any wildlife which, at that time, was quite taken for granted.

Islanders today, however, care little for Don Juan Vincente de Guemes Pacheco y Padilla Orcasitees y Aguayo Conde de Revilla Gigedo (yes, all that was his title), and prefer to relate the island name to the magnificent mammal.

While San Juan and Lopez Islands have, since the time of early settlement, had a history of bustling industry and agriculture, Orcas holds a long tradition as a vacation land. Ever since the 1890s, when ferries first made regular runs to the San Juans, mainlanders have flocked here to summer at gracious inns, or to "rough it" in canvas tents set up at beaches around the island. Several of the original inns have been modernized and are still in operation, while newer resorts have accommodations ranging from rustic beach cabins to modern apartments.

Orcas Island is served by the Washington State ferry from Anacortes (about a 1-hour trip), or from Sidney B.C., (about 2 hours away). The Orcas Island Airport, which is 1 mile (1½ km) north of Eastsound, is a daily stop on the schedule of San Juan Airlines. Charter air services also provide flights to the island.

Villages at Eastsound, West Sound, Deer Harbor and Olga have groceries, general stores and interesting little shops, while outstanding meals can be had at a number of restaurants. Daily or weekly lodging is available at resorts and inns; in summer, reservations are a must. The only public camping areas are at Moran State Park and the small hike-in campground at Obstruction Pass; resorts at Terrill Beach and West Beach also have some camping space.

The most extensive marine facilities are at Deer Harbor; a number of others are located on the other major inland waterways and along the northwest coast. Most have overnight moorages.

Bicycling is a favorite mode of travel on Orcas Island, as anyone can testify who has witnessed droves of bikes unload from a summer ferry. Orcas roads, however, are two-lane affairs with limited shoulders and plenty of ups and downs and curves. While traffic is often light, cyclists should use both care and courtesy when traveling here.

Don't let traffic back up behind a slow-moving party of cyclists—pull over at a safe place and let the cars go by. Travel in single-file and make yourself visible with a bike flag, reflectors, lights and light-colored clothing.

Nearly all island roads are black-topped and wind through forest and farmland, at times edging some of the many miles of shoreline. Water birds are sure to be seen, although in far greater number during the winter migratory season. A startled deer may dash across the road, then pause to stare back curiously at passersby. The greatest scenic sight of all, whether by bicycle, foot or car, is the drive to the top of Mt. Constitution in Moran State Park, and the culminating view out to a sea full of islands.

ORCAS FERRY LANDING

Access: Ferry to Orcas Island, boat
Facilities: Float, transient moorage, fuel, water, groceries, restaurant, shops

A small collection of stores, clustered near the ferry landing, caters to tourists waiting for the ferry and transient boats stopping by to fuel up and resupply ship's stores. The marina adjacent to the ferry landing is fully equipped to meet boating needs, while the grocery store has provisions for land or water visitors. A few gift and snack shops line the road on the slope above the ferry ramp, offering tourists pleasant places to while away their time while their cars sit in line, and to purchase a few remembrances of the island.

Most interesting of the buildings at Orcas is the white frame Orcas Hotel, overlooking the bay, attesting to the long-time role of the island as a resort center. Constructed in 1900, it began accommodating vacationers in 1904 and did a flourishing business for many years. Although it is still named the Orcas Hotel, it no longer has rooms to rent to tourists, but instead houses a restaurant and bar, while the upper floors are given over to business offices.

The limited parking space at the ferry landing has for years been a problem at Orcas during the hectic summer months, with a line of waiting cars often stretching for more than a mile up the road. A redesigned, spacious facility should replace this congestion sometime in 1979.

H. ORCAS ISLAND

KILLEBREW LAKE

Area: 13 acres
Facilities: Public dock
Attractions: Fishing, canoeing, bird watching

A lily-pad lake, its quiet waters reflecting cattails, skunk cabbage, pussy willows and fir trees along its margins. Although land bordering the lake is owned by the State Department of Game, there are no developed public use facilities. A short floating dock on the northeast shore provides the only access; the marshy nature of the shoreline limits any approach from other sides.

To reach Killebrew Lake, turn right immediately after leaving the ferry and follow the Killebrew Lake Road east. The road winds through thick forest, arriving in 2¾ miles (4½ km) at a Y intersection where Guthrie Road continues on the right, and the lake and a small pull-off are to the left. There is parking space for a number of cars along the pull-off; RV camping is permitted, although there are no toilets or water.

Boats must be hand carried for launching. Spend some time paddling about the lake, floating while watching the array of birds that live in the marsh, or fishing for the cutthroat trout which are stocked here. Boats with gasoline motors are not permitted.

GRINDSTONE HARBOR

No public facilities from either land or sea, but a favorite anchorage worth mentioning. Lying on the north side of Harney Channel, 2 nautical miles east of

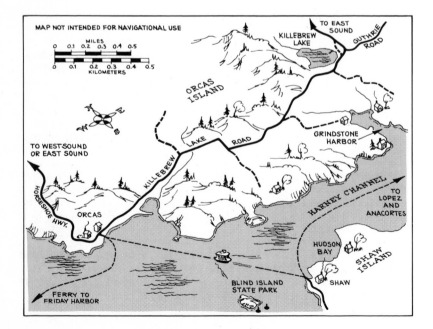

Killebrew Lake

the Orcas ferry landing, the small, deeply indented cove has space for just a few boats to drop a hook. Be wary of rocks lying in the middle of the channel at the entrance. There is ample depth for passage on either side of them.

The harbor received its name because Paul Hubbs, an early settler who lived there, owned a grindstone. He was often called upon to sharpen the axes, knives and other tools of the pioneers.

OBSTRUCTION AND PEAVINE PASSES

Among an entire album of scenic treasures, Obstruction and Peavine Passes rank as sublime. On clear days ferry travelers in Harney Channel are treated to the sight of the ethereal cone of Mt. Baker floating above the twin passes, with blue-gray layers of islands and hills stretching between.

Lying near the end of Rosario Strait, this doorway in the eastern wall of the San Juans serves boaters approaching the islands from Bellingham, which is 18 nautical miles northwest, and Vancouver, B.C. Obstruction Pass dog legs around Obstruction Island and has submerged rocks lying near the channel; Peavine Pass, on the south, while narrower, is easier to navigate.

A county boat launching ramp on Obstruction Pass provides the closest put in for small boats seeking access to the east side of Orcas Island, now that Doe Bay is closed to the public. To reach it, follow the road to Olga, turning east ¼ mile (⅓ km) before reaching Olga, onto a road signed to Obstruction Pass. Follow this road, turning left in another ¼ mile, then right in yet another ¼ mile.

H. ORCAS ISLAND

The road meanders down valleys and around hills, finally reaching Obstruction Pass about 2 miles (3 km) from the Olga Road intersection. The boat ramp and a small parking lot are between a volunteer fire station and a tall board fence of a private home. Property on either side of the launching facility is private.

Boats put in here can explore westward to the DNR campground at the point, and on into Buck Bay and East Sound. Westward and north are Doe Island State Park and Peapod Rocks. Brown Rock, lying in Obstruction Pass, is a bird sanctuary of the San Juan Islands Wilderness.

Currents in Obstruction and Peavine Passes can run in excess of 4 knots during flood, and heavy tide rips occur east of Obstruction Island. Use care in small boats.

OBSTRUCTION PASS CAMPGROUND

Park Area: **80 acres**
Access: **Boat or foot**
Facilities: **Campsites, picnic tables, fireplaces, toilets, mooring buoys,**
  no water
Attractions: **Boating, fishing, shrimp, hiking, beachcombing**

A forested point of land facing on Obstruction Pass gives backpackers and boaters alike an opportunity to camp in seclusion above a quiet beach. This Department of Natural Resources facility has nine camp sites scattered about a timbered flat, some within view of the water. If hikers wish further exercise after the walk in, a loop trail circles the area, through lush ferns and undergrowth.

To reach the trailhead to the campground, turn east off the Olga Road about ¼ mile (⅓ km) before reaching the town of Olga, onto the road signed to Obstruction Pass, which winds around an open valley, then circles a wooded hillside and heads south. As it curves east again, about 1½ miles (2½ km) from the Olga Road

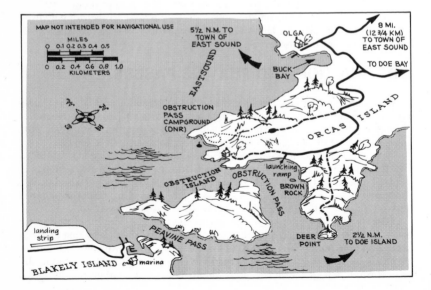

Explorer Scouts' survival training camp at Obstruction Pass Campground

intersection, a gravel road branches right. Turn onto this and follow it for 1 more mile (1½ km) to the parking area at the trailhead (space here for about fifteen cars); overnight camping at the trailhead is not permitted. The nearly level trail wanders through timber for ½ mile (⅓ km) to the campground.

By water, the park lies 1 nautical mile south of Olga on East Sound, and ½ nautical mile east of the boat ramp on Obstruction Pass. There are two mooring buoys in the bay, and space for several more boats to drop anchor in the sandy bottom. It's a pleasant spot, with a nighttime view of brightly-lit ferries in Harney Channel; however, during a strong southerly it may be a bit rough.

The pebbled beach slopes gradually into the bay, offering a fine place to draw up small boats. At low water explore tide pools along the rocky beach on either side of the bay.

DOE ISLAND STATE PARK

Park Area: 6 acres
Access: Boat only
Facilities: Campsites, picnic tables, pit toilet, dock with float, *no water*
Attractions: Hiking, fishing, beachcombing, scuba diving

Compared to the more spacious facilities of Sucia or Stuart or Jones Islands, Doe Island is a "mini-park", but it is a delight nonetheless. Located just arm's reach from the Orcas mainland, boats at one time could be launched at the nearby village of Doe Bay for a quick visit to the park. However, the Doe Bay resort is now a health institute and is not open to the public. At present the nearest boat launch area is on Orcas Island at Obstruction Pass, 2½ nautical miles to the south.

Deep draft boats should approach the island from the east, as a tide flat extends out from Orcas Island toward the west end of Doe Island. A dock with a

20-foot float lies on the north shore of the island; water depth at the dock is 8 feet at mean low water, adequate for most craft except at very low tide. Buoys placed in the channel between Doe and Orcas are private, not for public use; however, there is space to anchor. Small boats may easily be landed on the gentle beaches of the park's south side, but be wary of rocks just offshore.

Five campsites with fireplaces are spaced about the island; three in the timber, and two in sunny clearings just above the south shore, with views across Rosario Strait to Cypress Island. A latrine and garbage cans are located near the dock. No drinking water; you must bring your own.

A trail circles the island on the bank above the beach. On the south side the bluff has been undercut by waves, forming an interesting cave to explore. Gulls and other seabirds often gather on the wave-washed beach rocks, flying in startled flocks when approached too closely.

PEAPOD ROCKS

This mile-long chain of islets serves two "levels of interest". Below the sea is a State Parks Underwater Recreation Area, frequently used by scuba divers, while the grassy rocks protruding above the water are part of the San Juan Wilderness, attracting flocks of seabirds who congregate and nest here.

The underwater area from Doe Bay to Peapod Rocks is highly rated among scuba divers for its wide range of terrain and difficulty, from the protected waters of the bay to the deep, current-swept walls of the rocks.

The largest of the islands is North Peapod Rock, which has a navigational beacon. At the far end of the chain is, appropriately, South Peapod Rock, while stretched in between is an assortment of rocks which appear and disappear with the tide.

Landing boats on the rocks is prohibited, since such intrusion is disturbing to nesting birds. This is a favorite haul-out area for seals, and they can often be spotted sunning on the rocks or in the water nearby. Again, too close observation by man can startle the animals and cause them to leave their resting and warming grounds.

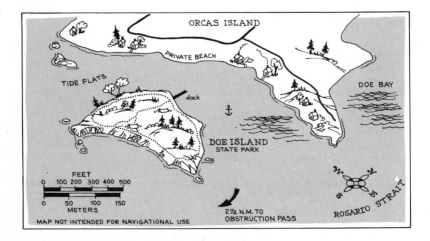

160

Doe Island beach

EAST SOUND

More than 7 miles long and a mile in width, the long, blunt inlet of East Sound nearly cleaves Orcas Island in two. Fjord-like hills rise steeply along the sides, suddenly dropping down to the flat at the head of the bay. It is a small inland sea in itself, with three ports-of-call, where sailors can spend hours cruising about its waters. East Sound is so large that it can "make its own weather", with winds funneling down the mountain-rimmed channel; it can be quite choppy here, but calm in outside waters.

With a smooth shoreline and beaches dropping off steeply, anchorages are few. Only at Buck Bay, Cascade Bay and at the head of the sound are waters shallow and protected enough to permit an overnight stay.

OLGA
Access: Ferry to Orcas, boat
Facilities: Float, transient moorage, groceries, restaurant

This small settlement on Buck Bay, near the mouth of East Sound, has a dock behind a log breakwater which provides some space for visiting boaters. Although it is owned by the Washington State Parks Commission, the dock is operated and maintained by the Olga Community Club, which charges a small fee for overnight stays. Shoreside amenities include a grocery store and an excellent restaurant.

In calm weather some anchorages are possible along the shore to the south. The lagoon at the head of the bay dries at low tide.

To reach Olga by land, follow the Horseshoe Highway north from the ferry landing through the town of Eastsound, then continue on the Olga Road through Moran State Park and south to the village. Total distance is about 17 miles (27 km). Olga is a popular sustenance-stop for bicyclists touring this end of the island.

H. ORCAS ISLAND

ROSARIO

Access: Ferry or airplane to Orcas Island, boat
Facilities: Docks, transient moorage on floats with electrical and water
   hookups, mooring buoys, fuel, groceries, launching ramp, boat rental and
   charters, restrooms, showers, laundry, hotel, motel, restaurant, coffee
   shop
Attractions: Boating, fishing, hiking, swimming (pool), sightseeing, historical
   landmarks, beachcombing

Unquestionably the most outstanding historical landmark of the San Juans,
Rosario has gained wide recognition as a fine resort and convention center. It
effectively combines the quiet grandeur of a turn-of-the century estate with the
slick posh of a modern marine resort.

The estate was built in 1904 by Robert Moran—twice Seattle mayor, shipbuilder, millionaire, man of unlimited talents and energy. Personal illness had
forced Moran to sell his shipbuilding enterprises in Seattle and retire to Orcas
Island. There he purchased land enclosing Cascade Bay on East Sound, and
designed and supervised the building of his mansion, Rosario.

Built on solid bedrock with concrete walls and inch-thick plate glass windows,
the fifty-four room main building required 6 years to complete; it is claimed that
2 years alone were consumed laying the parquet flooring of the interior.

The care lavished on the structure was also extended to the home's furnishings
and to the grounds of the estate. An organ with 1972 pipes, installed by Moran,
is still used regularly, and visitors still admire an imported stained glass window.
A figurehead salvaged from an old clipper ship was set up on the grounds and
remains there today, a symbol for this elegant resort. Carved in 1874 from a solid
pine log for the sailing ship America, the figure uses the motif of the Liberty
silver dollar of that period.

Moran left his mark not only on this quiet bay, but on all of Orcas Island. He
purchased large quantities of property on the island, and eventually donated
3600 acres of mountainous land, clothed with forests and lakes, to the state of
Washington to be used as the park which today bears his name. In addition, he
helped build roads, develop water systems and provided much-needed jobs for
islanders during the Depression years.

Following the death of his wife, Moran sold Rosario in 1938. Another ex-
mayor, Gilbert Geiser, formerly of Mountlake Terrace, purchased the property
in 1960 with the dream of turning it into a resort. With energy and expertise
which possibly matches that of Moran, he has transformed the unique estate into
a modern facility which attracts conventions, seminars and vacationers year-
around.

All of the original buildings of Rosario have recently been named to the
National Register of Historic Places, assuring their preservation in their original
state, with only necessary modernization.

To reach Rosario by land, follow the Horseshoe Highway east from
Eastsound, bearing right at an intersection 1 mile (1½ km) east of town. In 3¼
more miles (5¼ km), a prominent sign points down the road to the right to
Rosario Resort, 1¾ miles (2¾ km) away.

By boat, Rosario lies on Cascade Bay, halfway into East Sound, along the
eastern shore. Rosario Point reaches out to enclose the broadly curving bay, with

Trailhead to Rosario Lagoon at Rosario Resort

its jetty-created moorage basin. Buoys placed in the bay are for use of guests of the resort. Nearly any time of year it is necessary to have reservations for an overnight stay at the floats, or in the hotel. Boats unable to secure moorage can usually find space to anchor in the bay.

If guests become sated with the multitude of attractions that the resort offers, and feel the urge to stretch their legs, a trail leads up the steep hillside to the resort tennis courts beside Rosario Lagoon, where a trail can be followed to Cascade Lake in Moran State Park.

Walk past the concrete lagoon and generator building of the Rosario estate to find the trailhead—and what a trailhead! Every bit in keeping with the elegance of the resort, the rustic path is planked much of the way, and protected by a roof of cedar shakes. It zigzags up the hillside, through shadowed woods, stopping at a tiny pavilion, an ideal spot for resting, picnicking or a romantic tryst. The trail climbs steadily—rising 350 feet (110 meters) in about a mile (1½ km)—at times the aqueduct which supplies water for the generators of Rosario can be seen, along with the cascading stream which gives Cascade Bay its name.

Finally the trail emerges on a road near the dam at the end of Rosario Lagoon; tennis courts are to the left. Trails at either side of the dam circle the shores of the lagoon, reaching Cascade Lake and the park boundary in about ¼ mile (⅓ km). See page 166 for further state park trail descriptions.

H. ORCAS ISLAND

EASTSOUND

Access: Ferry or airplane to Orcas Island, boat
Facilities: Groceries, stores, fuel, hotel, restaurants
Attractions: Shopping, sightseeing, museum

Since the 1880s Eastsound has served as "business district" to Orcas Island. At that time the few little stores located here sold axes, seeds, flour, blankets and horsecollars to settlers, a blacksmith shod their horses, and a gracious inn provided meals and lodging to vacationing mainlanders. The town hasn't grown much since that time, in fact some of the original buildings are still there, but today there is a gas station instead of a blacksmith shop, the general store is stocked like any modern grocery store (although it still carries the hardware items necessary to island living) and the beautiful little Emmanuel Episcopal Church, built in 1886, still opens its doors on Sunday morning to worshippers.

As in early times, stores along Main Street and North Beach Road are interspersed with private residences, although some of these homes have been converted to shops selling antiques, arts, crafts and gift items to visitors. Outlook Inn, which still provides overnight accommodations and fine meals, advertises that it has been in operation since 1883, making it one of the earliest such establishments in the San Juan Islands.

One of the highlights of a visit to Eastsound is its interesting Historical Museum, located two blocks north of Main Street on North Beach Road. Four old log cabins, which were originally built elsewhere on the island, were brought to Eastsound and reassembled into the structure which houses the museum. Displaying a variety of construction from massive hand-hewn, dove-tailed boards to the traditional "round log" style, the building is nearly as interesting outside as is the collection inside.

The museum has an excellent display of Indian and pioneer artifacts and mementos from early island days. Many of the Indian objects were collected by Ethan Allan, the county superintendant of schools during the 1900s. Also on

Historical museum at Eastsound

Judd Bay and East Sound

display is Allan's hand-made boat, in which he rowed from island to island to visit the schools in his district. A recent addition to the museum is a shed behind the main structure which houses antique farm machinery.

By land, the town is reached from the ferry terminal by following the main road (Horseshoe Highway) north to the head of the sound, a distance of 8½ miles (13½ km). The Orcas Island Airport is less than 1 mile (1½ km) due north of the town, on the North Beach Road.

Eastsound's greatest drawback is that, even though it faces on a major waterway, it is difficult to reach by boat. The long, shallow flat at the head of the bay makes it necessary for large boats to anchor well out in Fishing Bay and dinghy to shore.

The possibility of a public marine park on Fishing Bay has recently been suggested. Such a facility, which would involve shoreland at the head of the bay, and possibly would include little Indian Island, which joins the mainland at low tide, would be an admirable addition to the town, especially if a dock with float and mooring buoys would improve boat access to businesses on shore.

A second saltwater park on Cresent Beach at Ship Bay, east of Eastsound, which was first suggested in 1978, has gained considerable support. The Crescent Beach site would provide a more nature-oriented park, with land access to a wide driftwood-and-sand beach and a marshy pond where birds congregate. Ship Bay, however, is extremely shoal, and boat access at this site would be unlikely.

Either of these parks would provide much-needed public recreational facilities on Orcas Island. As of 1979, however, the property being considered is still largely privately owned; when visiting Eastsound, do not assume that public intrusion on these lands is acceptable unless the area is clearly signed.

MORAN STATE PARK

Park Area: 4,934 acres
Access: Ferry or airplane to Orcas Island
Facilities: Campsites, picnic tables, picnic shelters, stoves, restrooms,
   showers, swimming beach, boat launch, row boat rentals
Attractions: Hiking, lake fishing, swimming, boating (gasoline motors not
   permitted), view tower

Drive, bike or hike—no matter how you get there, Moran State Park is a
"must see" for anyone touring the San Juan Islands. Oddly, though, on this
water-oriented island there is no easy way for boaters to visit the park. They
must be content with the many magnificent views of Mt. Constitution visible
from the waterways. From the northern reaches of Rosario Strait the lookout
tower on the summit is visible to the naked eye. Boaters can gaze up and admire
the scenic mountain and realize that landlubbers in the tower are admiring *their*
scenic craft cutting the blue waters.

The park is reached by ferry from Anacortes or Sidney to Orcas Island. From
the Orcas ferry landing travel north to the village of Eastsound, loop around the

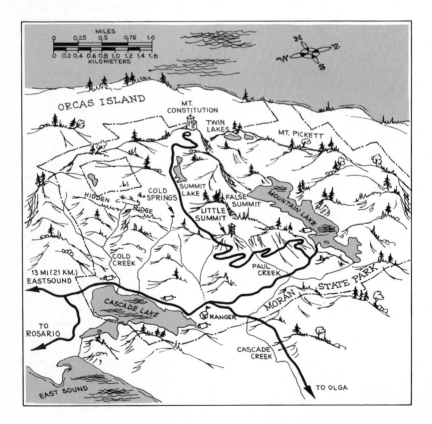

Cascade Lake trail

end of the sound and head south again. Roads are well signed. Distance to the park entrance is 13 miles (21 km). The island is popular with bicyclists, and although the steep Mt. Constitution road would severely tax an out-of-shape wheelman, many cyclists do make the trip to the top. Brakes must be in good condition for the downhill run. Drinking water is available at Cascade Lake and at the television station at the summit.

Fourth largest of the Washington state parks, 3600 acres of the land was a gift to the state in 1920 by wealthy shipbuilder Robert Moran. Additional land was acquired over a period of time by various means until today the park contains nearly 5000 acres. Much of the park development was done in the 1930s by Depression-era Civilian Conservation Corps.

Located on Cascade and Mountain Lakes are four pleasant campgrounds with a total of 137 campsites. A group camp near the south end of Cascade Lake accommodates large organized parties, by reservation only. Because of the ferry trip, many visitors to the park stay several nights, and campgrounds are often filled on weekends and holidays. Reservations are not accepted due to the vagaries of ferry travel; when campgrounds are full a notice is posted at the Anacortes ferry terminal. Doubling up is not permitted, so when Moran State Park is filled either go elsewhere on the mainland or telephone ahead from the ferry terminal to find accommodations at commercial campgrounds or motels on one of the islands. *In summer do not travel to the San Juans unless you are sure of overnight lodging.* Camping is not permitted at any place other than the established campgrounds.

Public areas in the park were completely renovated in 1978, insuring a pleasant stay for park visitors. Campsites were leveled, new stoves and picnic tables installed, water, sewer and wiring systems improved, and the rustic log buildings dating from CCC days were refurbished.

Many kinds of wildlife and birds can be seen occasionally near the roads and campgrounds and along the lake shore. Shy, black-tailed deer frequently cross roads; drive carefully to avoid hitting them. For the safety of wildlife and the convenience of other park visitors pets must be leashed and under control at all times while in the park.

For best wildlife viewing take to the trails and walk quietly, watching and listening for tell-tale movement, the chattering of squirrels and the calls of birds. There are no bears or poisonous snakes. Lake shore trails are excellent places to spot river otter, muskrat and raccoon, especially in late evening. Watch for burrows, tunnels and otter slides at the water's edge.

Nearly 30 miles of hiking trails lace the park. Most are enclosed by forest, but at times the timber opens and rocky, moss-covered bluffs protrude to give superb views north, west or south—Matia, Barnes, Clark, Lummi, Cypress, Blakely and Lopez Islands lie below, and on clear days, the snowy mass of Mt. Baker above and beyond.

Trail maintenance is done as crews are available from state and federally funded youth corps. Maintenance is sporadic on the less popular trails. In marshy areas brush and nettles may overgrow the path and in some spots downed timber may be encountered; park rangers can give information on current trail conditions.

Many trips are one-way, beginning at one point on the road and emerging farther along the road. Hikers who do not wish to retrace their route may be able to arrange transportation with a friend.

Cascade Lake

Drinking water sources on the trails are unreliable, especially in late summer; carry water on long hikes. When nettles and brush-beating are anticipated, wear long pants and carry a stick.

Do not build fires at any place other than in fireplaces at designated campgrounds. Fire hazard can be extreme, especially in the open meadows. Smoking while on the trail can be equally hazardous, so be sure all cigarettes are properly extinguished.

CASCADE LAKE

Usually the busiest place in Moran State Park, Cascade Lake boasts the park's three largest campgrounds and a day-use recreation center. All the campgrounds have spacious, level campsites with stoves and picnic tables. Restrooms and piped water are centrally located, with showers at Midway and North End Campgrounds.

North End Campground, with fifty-two campsites is ¼ mile inside the park's west entrance on a rise above the road and lake. A few hundred feet down the road are the picnic area and recreation center. Two large rustic shelters contain wood-burning stoves and ample tables for large group picnics; other tables are scattered in the trees and along the open lake shore. A float, diving board and shower for rinsing are available at a wide beach near the parking lot where summer swimming is supervised. Row boats are available for rent here; private boats may be launched at lower Midway Campground.

Midway Campground, ¾ mile farther south along the lake shore has fifty campsites lining both sides of the road, with some along the lake shore. Smaller South End Campground, located on a spur road around the far end of the lake, has seventeen campsites, some of them walk-in for bicyclists and backpackers.

Trout fishing is popular at the lake; the bridge across Rosario Lagoon, reached by trail from either end of Cascade Lake, is sometimes a successful spot. Observe State Game Department regulations on licenses, season and limits.

H. ORCAS ISLAND

FOREST RECOVERY DISPLAY

January 24, 1972, a violent storm with winds up to 100 m.p.h. racked the San Juan Islands. At Moran State Park hundreds of trees were downed, some of them century-old patriarchs. Park personnel spent months in clean up and repair of facilities and trails. Near Cascade Lake a 200 foot, 200-year-old Western red cedar which was toppled by winds has been left undisturbed as a reminder of the storm and an illustration of forest recovery.

Find the interpretive exhibit across from the recreation center near the start of the Cold Creek trail. A billboard display describes the storm. The giant tree is a progressive exhibit; visit it from time to time over the years to witness how nature, the original "ecological recycler", reclaims its own products.

CASCADE LAKE LOOP

This nearly level hike with ever-changing perspectives of the lake and mountain is enjoyable whether done only in part or walked as a 2½-mile (4 km) trail and road circuit.

Begin the hike west of the recreation center at Cascade Lake, passing through a marshy area bordered by a picturesque split rail fence, and along a rocky bluff where weathered Douglas fir frame the lake views and droop low over the water. At a fork less than ¾ mile beyond, the right hand trail, described in the following section, goes out of the park along the edge of Rosario Lagoon.

Another 300 yards down the lake shore a 50-year-old rustic log bridge spans the mouth of the lagoon. Farther southward along the lake are good views of the

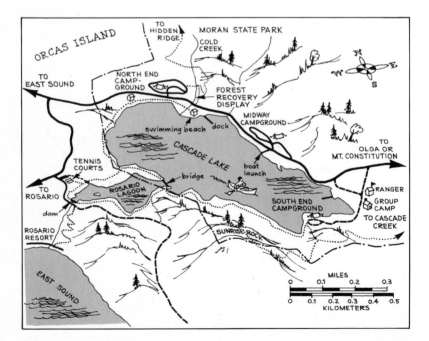

mountain summit. Belted kingfishers and shy, long legged great blue herons may be spotted along the shore; watch also for signs of muskrat and otter. Muskrat burrows, which resemble those of beaver, can be seen in the water. A large snail which is found in abundance along the shores of Cascade Lake is a dietary staple for these muskrats.

South End Campground is reached 1½ miles (2½ km) from the trailhead. Follow the road past the group camp and service buildings to the junction with the paved county road. Turn left (west) and walk the shoulder of the road back to the recreation center. Total distance around lake is 2½ miles (4 km).

ROSARIO LAGOON

Detour from the Cascade Lake loop onto a path by a quiet arm of the lake. The trail, sometimes used by fishermen, is unmaintained, but easy to follow. Hike the Cascade Lake trail around the north end of the lake to the unmarked trail fork ¾ mile from the recreation center. Rosario Lagoon can be seen through the trees on the right.

The trail leads out of the park near the lake shore. The quiet water is a popular stopover for migratory waterfowl—mergansers, goldeneyes, buffleheads and ring-necked ducks are but a few of the many colorful birds which call at the lagoon in fall, winter and spring.

As the trail nears the end of the lagoon, a jeep track goes straight ahead, terminating in a parking lot north of the Rosario Resort tennis courts. Continue left along the shore to a large concrete dam, ¼ mile from the Cascade Lake trail intersection. Many years ago Cascade Lake was only a large marshy area. Before the turn of the century the dam which created the lake was built to provide hydroelectric power for Rosario, below.

At the dam the trail reaches a paved road; walk down the road to the east side of the dam. On the right a trail can be seen dropping down the steep slope to Rosario before paralleling a wooden aqueduct. A small sign on the left of the road

Cascade Lake bridge

points to the trail which continues around the lagoon back into the park. If the route is lost in the brush at the outlet of the lagoon, follow closely at the water's edge until it again becomes clear.

Lake water laps at the hiker's boots; salal and swordfern crowd the trail. The Cascade Lake trail is rejoined at the log bridge. Total distance of detour loop around lagoon, about ¾ mile (1 km).

SUNRISE ROCK

For a steep climb to views down to the shimmering water of Cascade Lake and across to the lookout tower of Little Summit, find the Cascade Creek trail at the end of the road just west of South End Campground. In ¼ mile the Sunrise Rock trail branches right, drops slightly downhill, then begins the climb to the viewpoint, gaining 350 feet in ¼ mile. In the cool, virgin forest the trail passes several ancient Douglas firs nearly 6 feet in diameter which show the ravages of forest fires, lightning and woodpeckers.

Where the trail becomes sketchy, look for an apparent clearing in the trees around the hill on the right. A mossy ledge provides views of lake and mountain. Distance from South End Campground to viewpoint about ½ mile (¾ km); total elevation gain 400 feet (120 meters).

CASCADE CREEK

Flowing between Cascade and Mountain Lakes, Cascade Creek offers scenic waterfalls, woodland flowers and perhaps wildlife just a short distance from the road. Even novice hikers can negotiate the easy trails, although they are often muddy and sturdy shoes should be worn. The stream is closed to fishing.

The odd little water ouzel or "dipper" nests here along the banks of the stream. The plump, slate gray bird, slightly larger than a wren, dives into the swift flowing water and walks along the creek bottom to catch aquatic insects, invertebrates and small fish.

CASCADE FALLS

A chain of waterfalls on Cascade Creek can be reached by a short spur trail from the road, or may be viewed as part of a longer scenic jaunt from Mountain Lake to Cascade Lake. For the shorter trip, park at the trailhead on the south side of the road, ½ mile from the Olga-Mt. Constitution road intersection. Be careful not to block the service road which goes straight ahead. The trail sign on the right directs hikers first to Rustic Falls, however, the unmarked, overgrown road to the right of the trail sign can be followed directly to Cascade Falls in ½ mile.

Although the hike is well worthwhile any time of year, the falls are at their best in winter and spring when rainfall swells the lakes and streams. At Cascade Falls, the most spectacular of the four, the water fans widely across a 100-foot cliff, dropping into a tiny pool at its base. For a head-on view of the cataract cross the stream on slanting (and slippery) downed logs.

Cascade Falls

The trail switchbacks to the top of the falls, then levels out in the brushy valley of Cascade Creek, where salal and salmonberry overhang the stream. In spring find mushrooms and wildflowers along the trail—but by summer dense patches of nettles discourage off-trail wandering.

The upper falls are much smaller than Cascade Falls, but lovely nonetheless. Rustic Falls is 500 feet above Cascade Falls, and ¼ mile farther is the narrow plume of Cavern Falls. Just beyond Cavern Falls the trail merges with the dirt service road; continue on for ¼ mile to Hidden Falls, below the foot bridge at the Mountain Lake trail intersection.

The service road can be followed back to the parking area on the return trip. Total distance of loop hike slightly over 1 mile (1½ km); elevation gain 200 feet, (60 meters).

CASCADE CREEK TRAIL

For the longer hike from Mountain Lake to Cascade Lake, find the signed trailhead at Mountain Lake Landing, across from the ranger's cabin. The path heads south along the lake shore and passes a spur trail from Mountain Lake Road.

The concrete dam at the lake outlet is reached ½ mile from the trailhead; drop down the side of the dam to the wooden footbridge crossing Cascade Creek and turn right at a signed trail intersection at the end of the bridge. Downstream 200 yards is a pretty spot where the water cascades in foamy white rivulets and an unusual L-shaped bridge crosses the creek. At a third bridge at Hidden Falls, 1½ miles (2½ km) from Mountain Lake Landing, the Mt. Pickett service road is joined, then is abandoned again in another ½ mile where the main trail branches left.

Pause to enjoy scenic Cavern, Rustic and Cascade Falls tumbling down the slope. Sections of an old wooden aqueduct still in evidence at spots along the trail

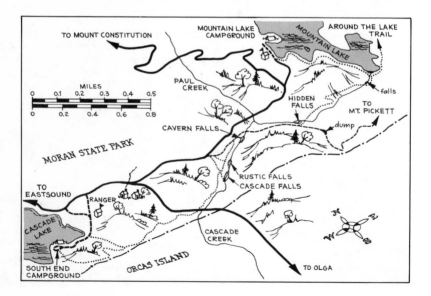

White-tailed deer at Moran State Park

are part of the park's original water system. The route crosses the Olga road near the south park entrance, 2 miles (3 km) trail distance from Mountain Lake Landing. Find the continuation slightly up the road to the west.

Cascade Creek heads southward out of the park, paralleling the road to Buck Bay, while the trail continues west through a timbered flat. Walk quietly and watch for Douglas squirrels, pileated woodpeckers and black-tailed deer in the open forest. South End Campground at Cascade Lake is reached 2¾ miles (4½ km) from the start.

Energetic hikers may wish to extend the hike by following the trail on the south side of Cascade Lake, arriving at the recreation center at the north end of the lake in another 1½ mile (2½ km).

MOUNTAIN LAKE LANDING

Lying a bit off the main thoroughfare, Mountain Lake does not receive as much tourist attention as does popular Cascade Lake. It therefore offers more solitude to those who are willing to leave their cars to enjoy its crystal waters and level shoreline.

To reach the lake, drive east from the park entrance to the Olga-Mt. Constitution road intersection. Continue toward Mt. Constitution; 2 miles (3 km) from the intersection a right-hand road fork is signed to Mountain Lake Landing. The road ends in ½ mile at a small parking lot.

The long lake fills a narrow valley between Mt. Pickett and Mt. Constitution. On the west shore, an 18-unit campground on a small peninsula overlooks the lake. A popular fishing spot, the lake contains several kinds of trout. Boats may be rented at the lake or bring your own for a tranquil paddle and magnificent views of Mt. Consitution. Launch boats on the north side of the peninsula at Mountain Lake Campground; gasoline motors are not permitted. Pack a lunch and go ashore on one of four small islands to spend some time with your thoughts.

MOUNTAIN LAKE LOOP

A nearly level 3½-mile hike circles the shores of Mountain Lake, highlighted by a unique view of the summit of Mt. Constitution. A counter-clockwise route around the lake is recommended so the prime veiws of the mountain lie ahead rather than at the hiker's back. The trail begins south of Mountain Lake Campground, contours the lakeside, and in ½ mile crosses the outlet of the lake on a bridge below a concrete dam. Just beyond the dam a right hand fork of the trail turns down Cascade Creek, with the main trail continuing straight ahead along the shore. The only appreciable elevation gain of the hike is midway around the lake where the trail climbs 50 feet above the water to skirt a rocky cliff.

The long summit ridge of Mt. Constitution rises above the lake. The fire lookout tower of Little Summit can be seen on the left and the stone observation tower of the main summit far on the right. Below the summit precipitous 1000-foot cliffs show their dramatic profile.

Look for bald and golden eagles, hawks and osprey soaring in the updrafts near the mountain. As of 1978, only three pairs of osprey were known to nest in the San Juan Islands, although others summer here. The same factors of population, pollution and pesticides which threaten bald eagles have severaly reduced the osprey population. Ospreys, which resemble small, white-breasted eagles, favor the heights of Mt. Constitution with its remote nesting sites and fish-filled lakes.

At the north end of Mountain Lake, 2¼ (3½ km) miles from the trailhead, a branch trail goes right to Twin Lakes. Continue along the lakeshore, with views

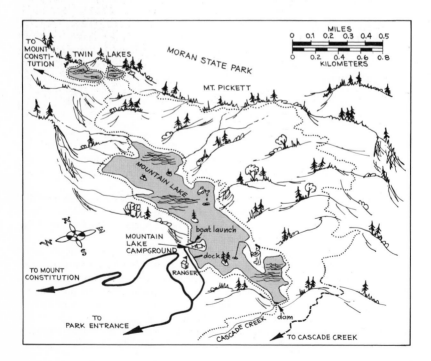

Osprey

across the lake to wooded Mt. Pickett, named for the commander of U.S. forces in the San Juans Islands during the Pig War.

Trail's end is reached at the parking lot at Mountain Landing, 1¼ miles (2 km) from the Twin Lakes trail intersection. Total distance of trip 3½ miles (5½ km).

TWIN LAKES

Tucked away on a timbered shoulder of Mt. Constitution, a pair of small lakes are the destination for one of the park's most pleasant hikes. During fishing season anglers will want to take along a fly rod to try for rainbow and cutthroat in the chilly spring-fed waters.

This trail and its continuation from Twin Lakes on to the summit of Mt. Constitution have been designated as the Bonnie Sliger Memorial Trail to honor a young woman who died in 1977 in a tragic fall at Doe Bay. She was a popular

YCC supervisor who had spent much time working with youngsters on trail maintenance in the park.

From the trail by the ranger's cabin north of the Mountain Lake Campground, the wide, level path meanders along the lakeshore for 1¼ miles (2 km) to the north end of the lake.

Leave the lake at a signed trail junction, following the Twin Lakes trail along a brook. In a stand of alder are scattered remnants of an ancient log cabin, possibly built by Civil War draft dodgers who are said to have lived in the area. Big Twin Lake is reached just short of a mile from the trail intersection. Total distance from Mountain Lake Landing to Big Twin Lake, 2½ miles (4 km); elevation gain 200 feet (60 meters).

Crude trails circle the shores of both lakes. Although usually not maintained, the trails are not difficult to find. Breaks in the enclosing timber permit glimpses of the summit of Mt. Constitution. Distance around Big Twin Lake about ½ mile, slightly less around Little Twin Lake.

MT. PICKETT TRAVERSE

A long trek on a rarely maintained trail may be used as part of an ambitious around-the-park excursion. Check with park rangers for information on current trail conditions.

Begin the hike at the Cascade Falls pull-out on the Mt. Constitution road, ½ mile east of the Olga road intersection. Follow the dirt service road east past Hidden Falls and the Mountain Lake trail intersection, and past a dump where park maintenance crews pile timber debris. The road climbs gradually, levels a bit at a flat near the south end of Mountain Lake, then begins to climb again in earnest, switchbacking up a steep arm of the mountain. Tall timber limits the views.

The 1750-foot (530 meter) summit of Mt. Pickett is reached 3½ miles from the trailhead. From here the route continues another 1½ mile to Little Twin Lake. The trail deteriorates considerably on the descent to Twin Lakes and route finding may be a problem, especially through marshy areas. Total distance to Twin Lakes 5 miles (8 km); elevation gain 500 feet (150 meters).

From Twin Lakes hikers may return to the road via the short but very steep trail to the summit of Mt. Constitution (1½ mile, 2½ km), or the gentle but somewhat longer Mountain Lake trail (2¼ miles, 3½ km).

MT. CONSTITUTION

Rising nearly ½ mile above the surrounding sea, Mt. Constitution is a dramatic landmark recognizable from many points throughout the San Juan Islands. The U.S. Exploration Expedition of 1838-42 named the mountain after the famous American frigate. East Sound was designated as Old Ironside Inlet, but that name did not persist.

From October to April the road is gated at the Olga road intersection at 5 p.m. During fishing season the road is closed above Mountain Lake, permitting anglers access to the lake. The road is kept open until 10 p.m. from June through August to accommodate late-day hikers and tourists who stay on the mountain to enjoy the magnificent sunsets from the summit.

Bench and compass at Little Summit

The Mt. Constitution road leaves the county road 1¼ miles (2 km) east of the main park entrance and in another mile begins the upward climb to the top of the mountain. With steep switchbacks and hairpin curves, it is not recommended for trailers, busses or large mobile homes. Halfway up, at the end of a switchback, are a pull-out space and dramatic vistas down to Cascade Lake, the twin summits of Entrance Mountain, East Sound and Spencer Spit on Lopez Island.

At Little Summit the road levels out and traverses the long summit plateau to the true summit. Total distance from park entrance to summit parking lot 6 miles (9½ km). Buildings and radio towers just below the observation tower are relay facilities for KVOS-TV, Bellingham.

LITTLE SUMMIT

Views that rival those from the observation tower on the higher main summit look down to Cascade Lake and Rosario Resort and out to the symmetrical humps of Entrance Mountain. Beyond are Shaw, San Juan and Lopez Islands, and far in the distance, above the Strait of Juan de Fuca, the Olympic Mountains.

As the Mt. Constitution road completes its last switchback and reaches the summit plateau, a signed pull-off east of the road provides parking space for a few cars. Walk 500 feet up the gated road to the tower and open viewpoint. The 40-foot wooden tower, which is a radio repeater and Department of Natural Resources fire lookout, is manned only in summer. Rest on the stone and log bench at the base of the tower and enjoy the scene, or wander across the open slopes for ever widening perspectives — lovely even on foggy days when mists swirl around the islands, encompassing, then suddenly revealing bits of the marine view.

H. ORCAS ISLAND

SUMMIT LAKE

This long, marshy lake near the mountain's main summit is only about 10 feet deep at its maximum. During winter it sometimes freezes over and islanders go ice skating here. There is only enough space to safely park two or three cars along the road where it meets the lake; be careful not to block or obstruct the vision of drivers.

Drop a canoe or inflatable boat into the water and commune with the frogs and explore the ½-mile lake, or drift quietly and watch for eagles, hawks and waterfowl. There are no fish. The marshy shoreline discourages hiking around the lake.

SUMMIT OBSERVATION TOWER

Perched atop the hard-rock summit of Mt. Constitution, the 50-foot stone lookout tower is one of the most unusual and fascinating features of the park. Children especially delight in climbing the many flights of stairs inside the tower, exploring the cell-like rooms, peering out the narrow window slits barred with wrought iron, and firing imaginary cross bows at imaginary armored knights (or laser guns at Wookies) in the forest below.

Designed as both a fire lookout and public observation tower, it is a facsimile of military fortifications built by mountain tribes in the Caucasus Mountains of Russia during the 12th Century. Orcas Island quarries supplied the sandstone blocks for CCC crews which erected the tower in 1936.

From the top, views spread in all directions. Look down to Twin and Mountain Lakes shimmering below, surrounded by dense green forest. Look out in all directions to the array of green and brown islands scattered in the azure waters of the sound. Especially striking is the geological pattern of the northern San Juans and Canadian Gulf Islands. Toy-like boats dot the water on clear days, their

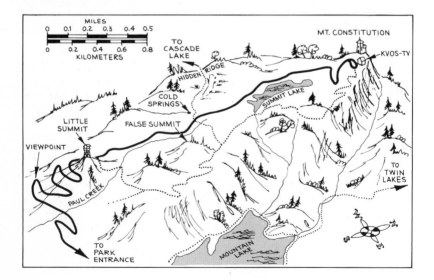

Mt. Constitution observation tower

silver wakes leaving long streaks on the smooth surface. To the east massive Mt. Baker looms, and to the south, through the smog of civilization, Mt. Rainier.

From the viewing area at the base of the tower glance over the stone railing for an added thrill—a dizzying view straight down the precipitous 1000-foot face of the mountain.

SUMMIT TRAVERSE

Hike from north to south along the mountain rim, looking downward to lakes and forest, outward to islands and sea. But take time to enjoy the quiet forest, too. The character of the vegetation changes rapidly from spot to spot as one hikes along the gradually sloping summit plateau. It is believed that the abrupt changes in the timber are caused by localized variations in the depth and permeability of the soil.

At one time a number of small ponds dotted the summit; many of these filled in with organic material and are now meadows. Hemlock and fir edge these

H. ORCAS ISLAND

former marshes, sustained by seeping water in the soft peat soil. In areas where sandy soil thinly covers the hard summit rock, crowded stands of lodgepole pine with shallow root systems grow only 15 feet high and 2-3 inches in diameter. Near the brow of the plateau where dirt lodges in the space between rock outcroppings, mountain hemlock and Rocky Mountain juniper with tenacious roots grow. Strong winds buffeting the face of the mountain twist these trees into beautiful Japanese "bonsai" shapes. In the valley of Paul Creek near Little Summit, moistness creates another forest type, the soaring big-trunked timber of Western red cedar and Western hemlock.

The signed trail departs from the south side of the turnaround loop at the top of the mountain behind the KVOS-TV buildings. Watch the route carefully at the beginning as there are several confusing side trails. After two switchbacks and a short traverse, a spur trail branches right 100 feet to an open rock with limited vistas to the south. The main trail descends steeply to a larger moss covered rock, ¼ mile from the start, with a 180° outlook encompassing the nearby summit cliffs and the distant mainland shores.

Views change as the route edges along the brow of the summit. The final scene is southeast down to Mountain Lake, then the trail turns west into the forest. At about ¾ mile a small stream crosses the trail; the dam at the outlet of Summit Lake can be seen through the trees on the right. The Cold Springs trail intersects in another ¼ mile, 1 mile (1½ km) from the summit trailhead.

Continuing southeast toward Little Summit, the trail descends to a grassy knoll with an eagle's eye view downward to Mountain Lake. Beyond here in ¼ mile watch carefully for another trail intersection which is signed, but could easily be missed. Avoid an old unused road going downhill slightly to the left, which eventually dead ends. The desired route to Little Summit turns right sharply at the intersection, contouring the slope.

The path, almost a road now, crosses Paul Creek and a short distance farther reaches Little Summit, 2¼ miles (3½ km) from the trailhead, 250 feet (75 meters) elevation loss.

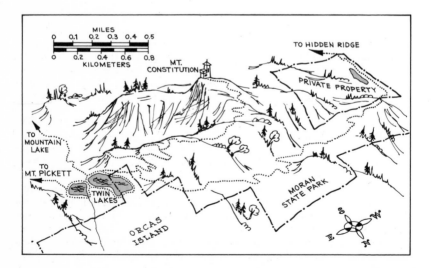

View from summit of Mt. Constitution; Lummi Island, Bellingham and Mt. Baker in distance.

MT. CONSTITUTION TO TWIN LAKES

One of the steepest trails in the park, losing over 1000 feet in a mile, but what scenery! Leave the hordes of car-bound tourists at the summit for challenging trails and rugged vistas.

Find the signed trail on the north side of the turnaround loop at the summit. After a few switchbacks it crosses a wooded flat and zigzags again down to an opening at the end of a switchback which looks north to Matia Island and Canada. The trail now turns eastward, traversing a saddle. Occasional glimpses through the trees of the craggy face of Mt. Constitution looming above.

At ¾ mile a short side trail on the right leads to an east-oriented rock outcropping, with the long profiles of Barnes and Clark Islands seen just below, Lummi Island farther in the distance and Mt. Baker on the horizon. Another ¼ mile down the main route a second spur trail leads right to the last viewpoint, the best one of all. Space here to rest and picnic, enjoying the wide views east and south—Mountain Lake, Obstruction Pass at the tip of Orcas Island, the mid-channel lump of Obstruction Island, thickly forested Blakely Island beyond, and to the far right an impressive view upward of the vertical summit cliffs.

More switchbacks, now reaching a gully with a signed trail junction; take the fork on the right, arriving at Big Twin Lakes in another 500 yards. Total distance from summit 1½ miles (2½ km), elevation loss 1240 feet (380 meters).

Pump house at Cold Springs

NORTH SIDE TRAIL

Swing wide around the north flank of Mt. Constitution through cool forest, past marshes and ponds. Views are few, but majestic eagles and hawks may frequently be seen in this oft-ignored section of the park. The trail is not heavily used and is rarely maintained; route finding in brushy areas may pose a problem.

Begin the hike on the Twin Lakes trail from the top of the mountain. At the trail junction 1¼ miles below the summit turn left onto the trail signed to Cold Springs. Immediately the route becomes vague and poorly marked, especially at two creek crossings. A section of trail which switchbacks upward to a small saddle was badly overgrown in 1978.

Just beyond a marsh the trail is clear again and a long traverse begins. Suddenly, an incongruous sight—a park bench of hewn logs beside the trail. Perhaps Robin Hood and his men gather here to plot their next foray against the Sheriff of Nottingham!

The trail climbs slightly, and 2 miles (3 km) from the trail intersection crosses first a rough dirt road, then a power line right of way. At this point the trail turns south along the edge of a section of private property within the park boundary. Beyond a lake and marsh the trail becomes sketchy again as it takes a short switchback up a rise. At a concrete post marking the corner of the private land the route again is evident as it turns southeast along the crest of Hidden Ridge.

The way is virtually flat now, through alder, fir and sword fern, to a trail intersection 4 miles (6½ km) from the starting point; bear left, continuing along the level plateau to Cold Springs and the road. Total distance 4¾ miles, (7½ km). Elevation loss from summit to Twin Lakes trail intersection, 650 feet (200 meters); elevation gain from intersection to Cold Springs, 350 feet (100 meters).

COLD SPRINGS AND HIDDEN RIDGE

A former campground, now an isolated picnic area in open forest, is reached by driving 3¼ miles up the mountain from the Olga-Mt. Constitution road intersection where there is parking space for a few cars at the gate and along the roadside. Just inside the gate is a rustic shelter with picnic tables and a stove, and south of the shelter (downhill) a round log and cedar shake gazebo shelters what was once Cold Springs. The old fashioned hand pump which supplied spring water was so frequently vandalized that park rangers gave up efforts to keep it operational. Picnickers must now supply their own water.

West of Cold Springs a trail wanders out to Hidden Ridge through a cool marsh with cedar, hemlock, deciduous alder and maple, thick ferns, and in season trilliums, skunk cabbage and marsh marigolds. Several ponds along the way are nearly dry in summer, but during the wet season offer sanctuary for migrating birds. The trail is broad and gentle for nearly a mile as it meanders the length of Hidden Ridge, then deteriorates when it continues around the north side of the plateau to Twin Lakes.

COLD CREEK TRAIL

Zigzag downhill, crossing and recrossing the branches of Cold Creek, or for a real workout begin at Cascade Lake and hike uphill, gaining 1700 feet (500 meters) elevation in 2 miles (3 km).

For the downhill route, find the trailhead by the round Cold Springs shelter on the south side of the picnic area. Hike west through the swampy flat to a trail intersection in ½ mile; bear left on the trail signed to Cascade Lake.

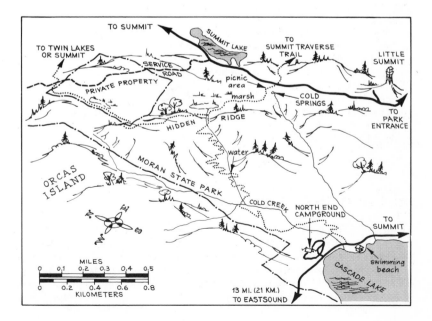

Moran State Park forest

As the steep descent begins, the vegetation immediately changes from wetland to dry, open forest. Curious squirrels edge head first down trees, circling out of sight around the trunk when they are spotted.

An open, moss-covered bluff ½ mile from the trail intersection is a good place to rest, snack and enjoy the view of Cascade Lake, Rosario Resort and points beyond. Aside from occasional glimpses of scenery through the trees while on the trail, this is the only viewpoint along the route.

Resuming the journey downward, the trail switchbacks to a crossing of the creek where a pipe spouts water for thirsty hikers. Drink now, for although the stream is recrossed several more times, the water may be fouled by hikers on the trail above.

In about 1¼ miles (2 km) the two branches of Cold Creek are crossed on log bridges. A traverse begins and the vegetation changes from open forest to tangled vine maple, berry bushes and nettles. At the end of the final switchback, just below the North End Campground, is an exceptionally pretty cascade across water-worn boulders overhung by ferns. Cold Creek is a natural spawning ground for native trout; fishing is not permitted.

Cascade Lake recreation center is reached 2¾ miles (4½ km) from the Cold Springs trailhead; elevation loss 1700 feet (510 meters).

AROUND THE MOUNTAIN

Although Moran State Park trails were designed for day hikes, and backcountry camping restrictions preclude tenting by the trail, a determined hiker can complete a circuit of the park by planning ahead to stay in one of the established campgrounds where the trail meets the road. Leave a car or tent in an unoccupied camp site to reserve the spot. It is desirable, though not essential, to pay the park ranger in advance for the site.

186

Two possible routes are listed here, although a number of variations are available. Hikers can choose the shorter, easier, scenic route, or opt for the more challenging, less-traveled outer loop which may involve some brush beating, trail finding problems, and along with it, more solitude. Either circuit could be completed in one day by a seasoned hiker, allowing little time for sightseeing. Refer to preceding pages of this chapter for descriptions of specific sections of trail. Carry water and, in case of backcountry emergency, a rucksack with the Ten Essentials: extra clothing, sunglasses, first-aid kit, extra food, flashlight (and extra cells), map, compass, matches, firestarters and knife.

Both hikes described here begin and end at the top of the mountain, with overnight stops at South End Campground on Cascade Lake. Cars may not be left overnight at the summit, so it would be necessary to park them at the campground and prearrange transportation up and down the road with a friend, or resort to the expedient of an extended thumb.

Elevation loss via each route on the first day is slightly over 200 feet (610 meters), all of which is regained the following day.

ROUTE A: THE SCENIC CIRCUIT

From the parking lot below the observation tower follow the Little Summit trail south and turn right onto the trail spur signed to Cold Springs. Follow the Cold Springs trail along Hidden Ridge to a junction in ½ mile. Head downhill to the Cascade Lake recreation center, cross the road and turn right onto the trail circling the north and west sides of Cascade Lake, finally reaching South End Campground, the first night's destination. Total day's distance is 5¼ miles (8½ km).

Begin the second day with the hike along Cascade Creek from Cascade Lake to Mountain Lake, reaching the dam at the Mountain Lake outlet. At the trail intersection turn right along the east side of the lake, and at the north end of the lake head upvalley to Twin Lakes. From the lakes climb the trail back to the Mt. Constitution summit. Total day's distance is 5½ miles (8¾ km); total distance of circuit is 10¾ miles (17¼ km).

ROUTE B: AWAY FROM THE MADDING CROWD

Begin the hike on the trail which descends to Twin Lakes from the observation tower parking lot. Just before reaching the lakes, turn left onto the trail signed to Cold Springs. The route swings around the northwest corner of the park, reaching the intersection with the Cold Springs trail. From the trail junction hike downhill to Cascade Lake, then turn right onto the trail around the north and west shores of the lake, arriving at the night's destination, South End Campground. Total day's distance is 7½ miles (12 km).

On the second day take the trail on the west side of the campground which is signed to Mountain Lake and follow it along Cascade Creek to the point where it joins the dirt service road. Follow the road past Hidden Falls and continue on the service road (which deteriorates to trail) over the top of Mt. Pickett to Twin Lakes. End the day by returning to the main road via the steep trail back to the summit. Total day's distance is 7¾ miles (12½ km); total distance of circuit 15¼ miles (24½ km).

WEST SOUND

Access: Ferry to Orcas Island, boat
Facilities: Marina, fuel, supplies, groceries
Attractions: Boating, canoeing, shrimp

The "middle" of Orcas Island's three major inlets, West Sound is both middle in size and middle in location, located between East Sound and Deer Harbor, running north for 3 miles to the base of the Turtleback Range. Prevailing northerly or southerly winds make the waterway a favorite with sailors who happily leave the busy traffic of Harney Channel for brisk sails up the sound.

The remarkable outline of the Turtleback Range, with the "shell" formed by 1500-foot Turtleback Mountain, and the "head" created by Orcas Knob, is quite easily seen from the waters of West Sound. Another good view of the turtle can be had from the north end of President Channel.

A long rock at the entrance to Massacre Bay, mid-way between Haida Point and Indian Point is marked by a daybeacon. At high tide considerable portions are submerged — give it a wide berth.

On the eastern "thumb" of West Sound is the village of West Sound, where there is a yacht club, marina and store, providing the only public access to the land in this area. The yacht club permits boaters to briefly tie up to their dock while shopping at the store. The marina has a hoist for launching; however, there is no public ramp in the area. Hand carried boats may be put in on the north shore of this "thumb" of the sound, where the road parallels the shoreline.

Boats planning to drop a hook for the night will find Massacre Bay quite shallow and open to southerly winds; the most protected anchorage is on the northwest side of Double Island, near the entrance to the sound.

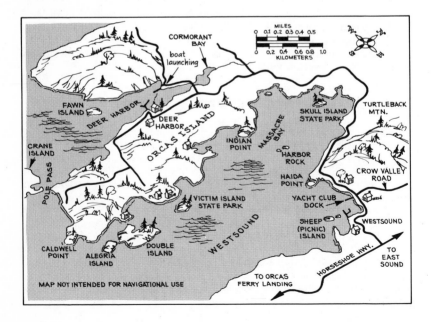

Turtleback Mountain from President Channel

To reach West Sound by land from the ferry terminal, follow the Horseshoe Highway north for 2½ miles (4 km) to the first major intersection and turn left. The town is reached in 1 more mile (1½ km).

The waterway offers little to the land-bound visitor, aside from the very scenic drive around Haida Point. Pretty little Skull Island is visible from the road near the head of Massacre Bay, but once the road rounds the head of the sound it ducks into timber and all marine views are lost.

In winter Massacre Bay fills with great rafts of all kinds of migratory waterfowl — buffleheads, scaups, goldeneyes, grebes and scoters — squawking and skittering about uneasily at every imagined menace from shore. When startled by sight of a human or stopping car, they depart in huge flocks of whirring wings, to alight farther down the sound.

INDIAN HISTORY

Lummi Indians claimed the San Juans as their tribal territory and large numbers of them summered here, gathering berries, bird eggs and roots of camas and other plants, then returning to the protection of mainland longhouses to wait out the dreary rains of fall and winter. Permanent villages were established on San Juan Island at Friday Harbor, Fisherman Bay on Lopez Island and West Sound on Orcas Island. The West Sound village, located at the head of the bay, was reported to have been named Elelung, and included a large, permanent longhouse. Temporary shelters were wooden frameworks covered with woven mats which were removed when the tribe moved elsewhere.

The bounty of the islands provided the Indians with all they required; fish, shellfish, deer, birds and other small animals for meat; berries and a wide variety of other plants for food (some nutritionists believe that the Coast Indians had a diet superior in vitamins to that which modern man has today); animal skins for

189

Migratory ducks on Massacre Bay

clothing; and an abundant supply of cedar trees which were utilized for nearly every purpose from homes and canoes, made from the wood of the trees, to clothing and baby diapers made from shredded bark.

With only the most basic of materials the Indians developed ingenious means of harvesting food. Nets and fishing lines were fashioned from incredibly thin strips of bark and plant fibers, which were braided for strength. Fish hooks had hinged barbs or gates to prevent the escape of the catch. At Pole Pass, between Crane and Orcas Islands at the mouth of West Sound, the Indians were known to stretch nets across the 200-foot channel, supported by tall poles (hence the name), to knock down low-flying flocks of birds. Reef netting, invented by ancestors of the Lummis, is still effective as a commercial fishing method today.

These Indians practiced the unusual custom of binding flat boards to the foreheads of their babies to permanently shape them with a broad, flat forehead and high crown. It is believed that a group of Coast Indians, traveling in the eastern prairies, were the ones that Lewis and Clark sighted, causing them to erroneously name the local Indians the Flathead Tribe, for the native Montana Indians were never known to practice the custom.

The local Lummis were generally peaceful people, content with the abundance of their land, however they occasionally suffered at the hands of war parties from the fierce tribes of the north, and would retaliate. Territorial acquisition was not the intent — such raids were primarily for the purpose of taking slaves, which were usually used later for ceremonial sacrifices, or killed at the whim of their captor.

The most vicious of these raids in recorded history occurred in 1856, when a party of Haida Indians from the north swept down on the West Sound village and slaughtered most of the inhabitants, taking the rest for slaves and completely destroying the settlement. More than a hundred Indians were reported to have been killed in the raid — since that time Massacre Bay has borne its lurid name.

SKULL AND VICTIM ISLANDS STATE PARKS

Park Area: Skull Island — 2½ acres; Victim Island — 3 acres
Access: Boat only
Facilities: None
Attractions: Picnicking, paddling, crabs

Skull and Victim Islands may be grisly names for such innocuous bits of land, but rather than any recent problem, they, along with Massacre Bay, recall the area's violent past history of bloody Indian raids.

Located only 400 feet (125 meters) off the shore of East Sound, Victim Island lies a third of the way up the sound, just north of Double Island, while Skull Island is near the head of Massacre Bay. There is no access to the parks from the nearby shore; small boats must put in at the village of West Sound, 1¼ nautical miles from either island.

The islands are small ("intimate" if you prefer) and rocky, with a few picturesquely scrubby trees. After a day of paddling exploration of the shore of West Sound, either is a fine spot to pause for a snack or a snooze. These are undeveloped parks, thus there are no amenities such as water, toilets or garbage cans. Fires or overnight camping are not permitted. Please take all garbage home with you.

The shoreline of East Sound wanders in and out, forming coves and bays ideal for small boat perusal. Sections of tideland at the head of Massacre Bay, south of Indian Point and at several other points around the sound are open for public use, up to the mean high tide level; stay off posted property.

Salal, a dietary staple of San Juan Island Indians. Berries were dried for winter use, leaves were smoked as tobacco and salal leaf tea was used as a medicine

DEER HARBOR

Access: Ferry to Orcas Island, boat
Facilities: Transient moorage with electrical hookups and water, fuel, boat
   launching, boat rental, supplies, groceries, stores, restaurants, restrooms,
   showers, laundry, swimming pool
Attractions: Boating, canoeing, sightseeing, shopping

Smallest of the Orcas Island inlets, Deer Harbor indents the western lobe of
the island for merely a mile. The village is a handy stop for boaters seeking to
avoid the long trek into East Sound for supplies, and is a tourist attraction for
both mariners and land-bound visitors.

Deer Harbor lies 6 nautical miles north of Friday Harbor, along a route
threading through the interesting "rock pile" of the Wasp Islands. Good anchorages can be had in the bay, although its extreme head is quite shallow. Wooded
little Fawn Island lies near the entrance; passage can safely be made on either
side of it.

To reach Deer Harbor by land, drive north from the ferry terminal to the West
Sound intersection in 2½ miles (4 km). Turn left here and follow the road as it
curves around the head of West Sound, then heads south to Deer Harbor, 4
miles (6½ km) from the settlement of West Sound.

Landlubbers and seafarers mingle in the shops and restaurants of the charm-
ing little town. Several of the neat clapboard buildings date from the 1890s,
when it was first established. Adding to the atmosphere, all types of interesting
boats tie up at the docks, ranging from shiny plastic runabouts to beautiful old
classic sailing vessels. The marinas have some boats available for rent.

Boats brought by land may be launched at the marina or at a trailered boat
ramp at the northwest corner of the harbor. To reach the ramp, turn west ½ mile
(¾ km) north of the village of Deer Harbor. The road crosses Cormorant Bay,
then turns south. When it curves west again, in about ¼ mile (⅓ km), a spur road
goes straight ahead, down to the water. Ample parking is adjacent.

Lagoon-like Cormorant Bay, extending north from Deer Harbor for another
½ mile, beckons to canoe and dinghy explorers. Kayakers with experience in
handling tidal currents can paddle the 2 nautical miles west to Jones Island State
Park, investigating Fawn Island en route, or can head southeast for 1¼ nautical
miles to Pole Pass, then on around Caldwell Point into the expanse of West
Sound. The current can be strong in Pole Pass; refer to a tidal current chart for
the best time to attempt the channel.

THE NORTHWEST SHORE

Access: Ferry or plane to Orcas Island, boat
Facilities: Moorage, boat launching, boat rental, fuel, camping, cabins,
   restrooms, showers, laundry

Here on this "outer shore" of Orcas Island, the gentle uplands roll smoothly
into the sea, interrupted only by small rocky points and the long finger of Point
Doughty. Broad sandy beaches provide some of the best recreation on Orcas

Deer Harbor

Island; however, there is no public shoreside facility in this area. Several commercial resorts have cabins, campgrounds and small boat facilities for vacationers. The resorts at Terrill and West Beaches provide boat launching ramps, equipment and supplies for boaters headed for offshore fishing grounds, scuba diving sites, or for a day's recreation at Sucia Island and points beyond.

Several generations of Northwest youngsters have had their first taste of the San Juans at the YMCA Camp Orkila which is on the west shore, just south of Point Doughty. Since 1906, when the camp was founded, up to 3000 children each year have fished, swum, beachcombed, sailed, canoed, hiked, ridden horses and had wilderness campouts here, and have grown to love the islands.

Resorts along the shore are reached by land from several roads branching from East Sound and the Crow Valley Road. All are well signed. By boat, West Beach is 10 nautical miles northeast of Roche Harbor, while the resort at North Beach is 3 nautical miles farther.

Small boats or canoes launched at Terrill or West Beach can spend hours investigating the shoreline, stopping at Freeman Island and Point Doughty. Sucia Island is a tempting destination, lying only 2 nautical miles north of North Beach; however, it is recommended only for those experienced with open water hazards, for there are reefs and tide rips along the way.

These very reefs and tide rips make this a popular salmon fishing grounds, where many anglers troll during the summer months. The deep channels of offshore reefs attract scuba divers who dive from boats at Parker Reef, Point Doughty and throughout President Channel, finding abalone, swimming scallops and exceptionally large lingcod and cabezon. Free diving and snorkeling are good near the docks and bays of the resorts, and on a series of rocky ledges between Freeman Island and the Orcas shore.

Harbor seals

POINT DOUGHTY

Access: Boat only
Area: 60 acres
Facilities: Picnic tables, fire rings, camp sites, pit toilet, *no water*
Attractions: Fishing, scuba diving, tide pools, beachcombing

Not an appealing anchorage, with kelp beds, tide rips and submerged rocks in the vicinity, but for small boats that can be hauled up on the beach, Point Doughty offers go-ashore camping near some of the best scuba diving to be found in the Northwest.

This Department of Natural Resources area is accessible to the public only by boat. A public trail from above was proposed at one time, but the idea was abandoned for fear that heavy public use of such a trail would disturb eagles which nest in the area. An overland path does reach the point from YMCA Camp Orkila, down the beach to the south, however that route is restricted to use by youngsters from the camp.

A few campsites perch on the grassy slope above the beach, with stunning views across President Channel out to Boundary Pass. Offshore rocks can make landing boats at the beach a bit tricky; be prepared to wade.

FREEMAN ISLAND STATE PARK

Park Area: Less than an acre
Access: Boat only
Facilities: None
Attractions: Beachcombing, tide pools, scuba diving, fishing

This undeveloped state park is an eroded, narrow ridge of an island, with a fringe of gnarled old trees. Perhaps eventually it will all wash away, but for now enjoy the meager little island, made beautiful by the ravages of weather and time.

Freeman Island State Park

Freeman Island lies just 300 yards (275 meters) off the west shore of Orcas Island. Boaters frequently take day excursions to the island from West Beach Resort, Beach Haven or Camp Orkila, a YMCA youth camp, all less than a mile (1½ km) away.

The shores are very rocky; boat landing is best on the south side and west end. Scuba divers often dive in the reef extending to the west.

Fires or overnight camping are not permitted. Please do not litter; if you picnic take your garbage home with you.

SKIPJACK AND BARE ISLANDS

Lying only 4½ nautical miles from the northwest shore of Orcas Island, Skipjack Island has in the past been a popular destination for small boat adventurers. The island, however, along with Bare Island, ¾ nautical mile to the east, is one of the wildlife refuges of the San Juan Islands Wilderness, and is now closed to any public use. Any landing on the island is prohibited, except by special permit.

The islands support large rookeries of glaucous-winged gulls, pigeon guillemots, tufted puffins, auklets and other pelagic birds. As man's use of the other San Juan Islands increases, it is vitally important that some of these lands be reserved exclusively as refuges. *Any* intrusion by man, no matter how cautiously done or well-intentioned, can frighten birds from their nests, leaving their eggs and young open to predation by rival birds. Even after the nesting season, it is important that the birds have rocks on which to rest undisturbed.

The waters south and east of the islands are popular salmon fishing grounds, and the long underwater reefs nearby are popular with scuba divers. Boaters engaged in these activities should stay as far away from the islands as possible.

WALDRON ISLAND

Waldron is a staunchly individualistic island, defying categorization, either physically or socially, with any other San Juan. In fact, it is "lumped" here with Orcas Island only due to its close location, only 2 nautical miles west of Orcas' West Beach, not because of any basic filial relationship.

The people, too, of Waldron display this same individualism, along with a strong sense of self-sufficiency, for the island has no electricity, telephone, or regular ferry service, and most residents prefer it that way. This is not a totally primitive island, however, for many homes are modern, with private generators to power lights, radiotelephones and appliances, while refrigerators and stoves operate on propane.

One of the most unusual pieces of topography to be found hereabouts, Waldron resembles a huge, flat skate (fish), with one wing tip flipped high in the air. More than half of the island is a marsh and meadow flatland covered with glacial drift, rarely more than 100 feet in elevation, while at the southern tip, the cliffs of Point Disney suddenly rush upward to a height of over 600 feet. The imposing, fortress-like walls display beautiful banding of exposed layers of sandstone and conglomerate.

The island has less than a hundred residents, with most homes located along the two broad bays of the northwest shore. The "village" of Waldron consists of several abandoned buildings huddled around a dock on Cowlitz Bay. Passing boaters rarely stop here, as there are no onshore facilities, and the open bay is a marginal anchorage, even in good weather. Mouatt Reef, which is exposed at low tide, lies at the entrance to the bay, 300 yards off the end of the dock.

The islands only other harbor is rock-bound Mail Bay on the east side, which in early days was the local mail stop, and is sometimes still used today by the mail boat when the seas are too rough at Cowlitz Bay, obviously believing that "neither rain, nor sleet, nor snow, nor towering seas. . ."

The Nature Conservancy has purchased 273 acres of beach, meadow and marshland on the west side of Waldron Island, facing on Cowlitz Bay, in order to preserve it in its natural state. While this land is open to public use, it must be emphasized that this is a biological preserve, not a recreational area; camping and picnicking are not permitted. It is urged that the area be visited only by those seriously interested in viewing and studying the birds — and such a magnificent assortment of birds it is!

Douglas fir, oak and madrona forests attract colorful goldfinches, Western tanagers, red crossbills and nuthatches, while red-winged blackbirds and long-billed marsh wrens and myriad other marsh birds inhabit the wetlands. Ponds are resting grounds for migratory fresh-water ducks, and occasional groups of majestic long-necked whistling swans.

Eagles nest in the forested heights of the island, as well as across President Channel on Orcas Island. The nesting sites are carefully protected by island residents and conservation organizations.

EAGLES

A black silhouette with 6-foot wing span, soaring, wheeling in the summer sky, its white head glinting in the sun, then suddenly swooping downward to alight in a skeletal tree snag — a bald eagle is one of the most spectacular sights in

Bald eagle in the San Juans

the San Juans. At times they seem so common that tourists become blasé about them, but those who understand the significance of their presence can never fail to be thrilled by sightings of these elegant raptors.

The San Juan Islands have the largest, and healthiest, concentration of nesting bald eagles in the continental U.S. About thirty pairs are known to breed here, leaving the area only in the fall when spawning salmon lure them up inland rivers. Other migratory bald eagles summer in the islands, after nesting in Alaska and coastal British Columbia. Golden eagles are also commonly found in the San Juans, although they are not known to nest here; with stronger territorial drives they prefer more expansive aeries in the inland mountains.

Immature bald eagles are often mistaken for golden eagles, for they do not display the characteristic dark body and snowy head until their third or fourth year; however, the young bald eagle is evenly brown-colored, with some white mottling as they mature, while the golden eagle displays distinctive patches of lighter colored feathers at the base of the tail and in the wing linings at the base of the primaries.

It is remarkable to find such a concentration of these strongly territorial birds in one area, along with large numbers of hawks, vultures, owls and other predators with competitive feeding requirements. With the bountiful supply of rabbits, fish and other favorite tidbits, the isolation of the islands and the current protective attitude of the human residents, the eagles have modified their customary behavior to a more social existence. While golden eagles do take large numbers of live rabbits, and thus are valuable to the islands in the control of these prolific rodents, bald eagles prefer fish and carrion.

Eagles, which may be seen almost any place in the San Juans in spring and summer, even sometimes near such busy places as Roche Harbor or Sucia Island, can be spotted in snags of forested areas, gliding low over the water of quiet bays, or rising in concentric circles in thermals above mountains.

Several San Juan residents, assisted by the Nature Conservancy, have attempted to locate all bald eagle nesting sites in the islands, and have taken steps to protect them by obtaining conservation easements of 20 to 40 acres as a "buffer zone" around each nest tree, to prevent logging or public disturbance of the site. The trees are surveyed by air each year to determine activity. In 1978, thirteen chicks were believed to have been successfully raised in San Juan nests.

In addition to the serious threat of loss of nesting sites by human encroachment, the birds also succumb to such natural hazards as storms, disease and predatory raccoons, crows and hawks. Although they are placed on the list of endangered animal species, and are protected from being killed (except in Alaska), they are occasionally shot by irresponsible hunters.

Still another threat to these majestic birds is now the poisons in the environment. Since they have exceptional longevity, being known to live up to thirty years in the wild, all of that time absorbing agricultural and industrial toxins in air, plants and water, and in addition eating large quantities of carrion which may itself have died as a result of such poisoning, the eagle's bodies become storehouses of DDT, dieldrin, PCB's and mercury. These poisons, if they do not kill the bird outright, can cause sterility, thinning of egg shells, failure of eggs to hatch and weakened chicks, ending the reproductive capabilities of the adult.

The bald eagle is so perilously close to extinction, it is imperative that they be given every possible protection if the species is to survive. Visitors to the San Juans should stay well away from nesting sites, enjoying the birds from a distance with field glasses.

Bald eagle nesting sites are selected with a definite thought to overseeing of territory. The tallest of trees is chosen, and a platform of sticks, moss, shredded bark and mud is constructed. Nests are reused from year to year, and eventually are used by their offspring. Each year the nest is redecorated and expanded with additions of sticks and mud until, over a period of decades, they can become many feet across and weigh more than a ton. Such huge nests have been known to come crashing down during storms, or to fall from their own sheer weight.

In the San Juans, the elaborate pre-nuptial rituals may be observed in February. During courtship, groups of eagles circle high in the sky in mock combat. A male separates from the group and dives into the forest, snapping a branch from a tree and bearing it upward to his intended mate. The branch is passed to the female and, talons entwined, the pair tumbles earthward in a wild cartwheel, separating only moments before impact.

One to three eggs are laid in the nest, and in early April the downy chicks appear, although usually only one will survive. While a female may desert her nest if disturbed during the incubation period, she rarely will abandon it once the eggs are hatched.

In about twelve weeks (about mid-July), the young have feathered out and are ready to leave home. Just prior to this time they can sometimes be seen teetering awkwardly on the edge of the nest, exercising their wings.

Nesting eagles in the San Juans have been known to be quite accustomed to human residents, but become agitated by the presence of strangers. The best means of viewing them is from inside a car or boat, with binoculars.

I. THE NORTHERN BOUNDARY

Dotting the sea like the scattered gems of a broken necklace, a scenic string of four groups of islands — Patos, Sucia, Matia and Clark — form the northern boundary of the San Juans. Although early settlers lived on the larger of these islands from time to time, none were ever officially opened for homesteading. In early days cobblestone was quarried on Sucia, and later foxes were commercially raised on Sucia and Matia.

During the late 1800s, after the settlement of the boundary dispute, the U.S. government set aside the region for coastal defense, but when modern warfare made this concept obsolete, many of the islands were converted to wildlife sanctuaries and state marine parks. Sucia, made available for private development in the 1950s, was purchased in part by the state and part by boating clubs, under the leadership of Ev G. Henry, and turned over to the State Parks and Recreation Commission for development as a marine park.

These two dozen islands and rocks share a common geological history. Tilted beds of shale and sandstone, believed to have been deposited as a river estuary during the Cretaceous Period, 65 million years ago, were covered by layers of gravelly till from glaciers which twice covered this region in more recent times. Sea animals such as clams, snails and ammonites which were buried in the sediment of the estuary became the well-known fossils of Fossil Bay. Erosion of the folded beds of alternating hard and soft material accounts for the long parallel ridges enclosing slender bays. The glacial till provides good support for vegetation, thus the larger islands are thickly covered with trees and brush.

Sandstone beds exposed on the edges of the islands have been eroded to fantastic shapes and patterns lovely enough to make a sculptor envious. Caves formed were used by early day smugglers and today delight beach explorers. The pitted rocks provide nesting areas for a variety of pelagic birds, while seals haul out on the smooth, sun-warmed rocks of the more secluded beaches.

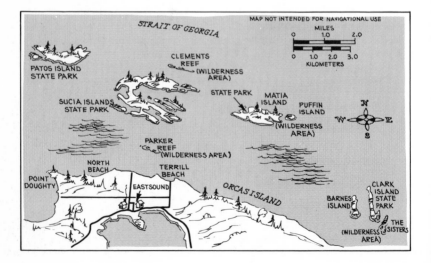

Madronas at Clark Island State Park

Matia beach

Accessible only by boat, the nearest put-in for small craft is at Terrill Beach on Orcas Island, where boats also may be rented. Sucia, the closest landfall, lies 2 nautical miles across the channel. In a small or unpowered boat, crossing at slack tide is recommended with a careful eye to the weather. Tidal current in the channel can be strong, and rough water may occur near the middle, at Parker Reef.

Once Sucia is reached, small boaters can island-hop, timing their open water ventures for favorable tides. Active Cove on Patos Island is 2½ nautical miles northwest of Sucia's Shallow Bay. To the east, Matia Island lies 2¼ nautical miles from Fossil Bay on Sucia, while Clark Island is southwest 4 nautical miles farther. Kayakers should not attempt these trips unless trained and experience in ocean paddling.

PATOS ISLAND STATE PARK

Island Area: 209 acres
Park Area: 207½ acres
Access: Boat only
Facilities: Campsites, picnic tables, pit toilets, mooring buoy
Attractions: Clamming, scuba diving, fishing, beachcombing, tide pools

Patos Island, the northern outpost of the San Juans, commands sweeping views of boundary waters and Canadian lands. A lighthouse occupies the western tip, Alden Point, while the remainder of the mile-long island is a marine state park. On the eastern end parallel ridges of erosion-resistant rock extend far out into the water, like toes on a foot, hence the name Toe Point. Slightly removed from the boating mainstream and lacking the many protected anchorages of Sucia and Stuart, Patos attracts fewer boaters and the beaches are uncrowded.

Patos can be reached only by boat; the nearest launching area is at Terrill Beach on Orcas Island, 5 nautical miles across President Channel. The east

entrance to Active Cove, the only protected harbor on the island, is filled with large rocks, so entry should be made from the west. Heavy tide rips occur on the north side and around Toe Point.

The deep, narrow cove holds a single mooring buoy and has room for a few additional boats to anchor. At the head of the cove on a grassy spit is a pleasant camp area with picnic tables and space for a few tents. A popular scuba diving area, the sandy beaches at Active Cove and Toe Point offer clamming and beachcombing. The area around the unmanned lighthouse is posted for "Authorized Personnel Only".

Eroded sandstone cliffs edge the south side of the island, making beach walking difficult there; however, an unmaintained cross-island trail leads to the gentle shores on the north. To find the trail, follow a dirt service road west toward Alden Point. Avoid the trail which branches right about 30 feet past the toilets. Although that trail heads eastward down the center of the island, it fades in heavy brush midway and only determined brushwhacking through salal and maple can lead to the end of the island.

On the service road, about 50 feet before the posted lighthouse boundary, an unmarked trail branches northeasterly. In a short distance the trail passes the tumbled-down remains of a shack and continues on through thick brush to the north shore in about ¼ mile. Note carefully the spot where the trail emerges on the beach, or mark it with a rock cairn for the return trip. The beach can be followed all the way to Toe Point, investigating tiny coves along the way. Watch for seals fishing the tide rips off shore.

Patos Lighthouse was established in 1893; the present structure was built 15 years later. The light is now automated, as are all such warning devices throughout the San Juans.

Patos Island is the setting for Helene Glidden's book **The Light on the Island.** Mrs. Glidden lived here as a child at the turn of the century when her father was lighthouse keeper; her book is based on her childhood adventures and the early history of the San Juans. The vivid accounts of smugglers, Indians, visits by "Colonel" Teddy Roosevelt, rowing to Bellingham in a skiff, and the day-to-day routine on this far outpost give readers insight into early life in the islands. The book is now out of print, but is available in many public libraries.

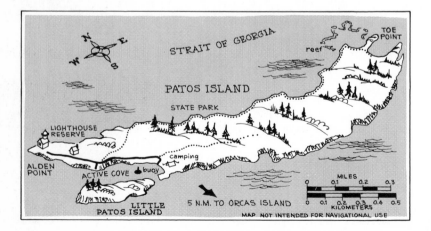

Sucia Island from Strait of Georgia; Orcas Island in distance 205

SUCIA ISLANDS

Islands Area: 749 acres
Park Area: 562 acres
Access: Boat only
Facilities: Campsites, picnic tables, picnic shelter, stoves, water, pit toilets,
    docks with floats, mooring buoys
Attractions: Beachcombing, fossils, clams, crabs, swimming, hiking, fishing,
    scuba diving

Mile-long rocky fingers protecting shallow bays form the group of eleven islands known as The Sucias. Over a 20 year period, beginning in 1952, portions of the present park land were purchased by the state for recreational use. During the 1960s, 319 additional acres were bought by the Puget Sound Interclub Association of boaters and entrusted to the care of the State Parks and Recreation Commission for use as a marine state park. All of Sucia Island, Little Sucia, Ewing and the Cluster Islands are now park property. The Finger Islands in Echo Bay and tiny Harnden Island at the mouth of Mud Bay are privately owned. With nearly 9 miles of waterfront, six bays and extensive boat and camping accommodations, Sucia Island State Park provides one of the best public marine recreational facilities in the San Juans.

Located 2 nautical miles north of Terrill Beach on Orcas Island, the nearest point where boats can be rented or launched, Sucia is inviting to boaters in vessels ranging from kayak to luxury yacht. Two docks with floats in Fossil Bay

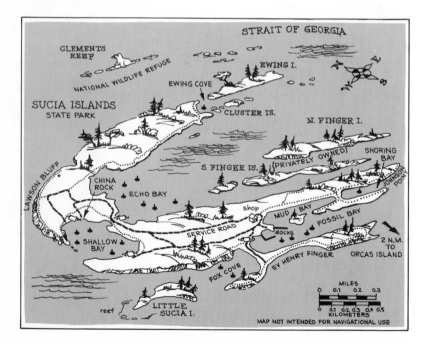

Fossil Bay

and forty-eight mooring buoys scattered around the island are heavily used by boaters. Small boats can be beached at any of the bays.

Boaters in small craft will need to exercise caution enroute, carefully considering the weather and tides. Heavy summer traffic or larger boats can also be a hazard. The trip is recommended only for experienced ocean kayakers and canoeists.

During summer, facilities can be very crowded at Sucia. During 1977, 129,000 boaters used the park, an increase of 300 per cent over 1971, and usage continues to grow. Be prepared to anchor if necessary or go elsewhere if unable to secure a safe moorage. Buoys and floats are first-come, first-served and the practice of "reserving" a buoy by tying a dinghy to it for the later arrival of a friend or for the return of the mother craft is neither courteous nor legal; it can result in your tender being cast adrift.

The Spanish name Sucia is correctly pronounced Su-*see*-ah, although few people, even local residents say it that way. The common pronunciation is *Sue*-shuh — not as melodious, but perhaps more logical to an Anglicized tongue. The name, meaning "dirty" or "foul water", was given to the island by early explorers who noted the dangerous rocks and reefs near the shores. Boaters today should take warning from the name and be wary of submerged rocks offshore and in the bays. Deep draft boats should be especially careful that they have enough depth in the swing of their anchorage during low tide.

Sucia has some of the finest examples of eroded cliffs typical of these northern islands. The rocks are sculpted by the chemical action of salt water on sandstone, assisted by the wearing action of wind and waves. Low level wearing of the beaches here and on many of the other San Juan Islands is limited by tide rips

Water-worn rocks at Fox Cove

offshore. Only at high tide do storm waves reach shore without being broken up by the tide rips. Benches at the high tide level demonstrate the cutting action of the waves.

The fierce wave action can occasionally present problems to boaters at Sucia. Be particularly careful when a southeaster blows into any of the bays on the southeast side of the island.

The fashion once was to spray-paint the name of visiting boats on the sandstone cliffs of the island. All this graffiti has recently been cleaned from the rocks. The fad, hopefully, is now past, so that today all visitors can enjoy the natural beauty rather than the ugly scrawls of insensitive yachtsmen.

SUCIA BAYS

Fossil Bay is the hub of park activity, with its floats and buoys filled nearly every night of the summer season. Campsites with water, picnic tables, stoves and a small picnic shelter can be found in the sparse trees near the docks, while more are nearby on the sandspit between Fossil Bay and Fox Cove.

Mud Bay, offset from Fossil Bay, nearly empties at low tide; other times the water is just deep enough for dinghying. Harnden Island at the entrance to Mud Bay is private property.

More camping areas are situated around the island at Echo Bay, Shallow Bay, Snoring Bay, and Ewing Cove, for a grand total of fifty-one sites. In summer drinking water is available at Fossil Bay, Fox Cove and Shallow Bay; however, from November through March all but the Fossil Bay water pipes are shut off to avoid their freezing.

Across a low sand spit from Fossil Bay, Fox Cove faces westward, sheltered by Little Sucia Island. Worn cliffs on the north side of the bay form marvelous shapes, including an 8-foot rock mushroom where children can pretend at Alice in Wonderland. The sandy beach at the head of the cove is the best in the island for wading and swimming.

Row out to Little Sucia Island from Fox Cove for a private picnic and evening views of blazing sunsets. Currents in the channel between the islands can be strong; use care. Little Sucia is primitive, with no formal trails. Fires or overnight camping are not permitted.

Tiny Snoring Bay on the south side of Johnson Point, generally scorned by power boaters, is a haven for paddlers seeking refuge from the noise and fumes of motors. The bay received its name when park officials visiting the island discovered the ranger there enjoying a siesta. Snoring Bay has two moorage buoys and two campsites on shore.

Indenting the western end of the horseshoe-shaped island, Shallow Bay has three distinct sandy beaches with a campground on each, separated by rocky headlands. Enter the bay with care as submerged rocks protrude out from the points at either side of the entrance. Eight buoys and numerous good anchorages attract boaters, however the bay is extremely shoal; check your depth and the predicted tides before settling down for the night.

Shallow Bay offers driftwood, clams and crabs to beachcombers. Large cockles may be picked up right on the surface at low tide, while other clams hide deeper in the sand. Dungeness crabs, which lurk in the eelgrass of the cove can be trapped with crab pots in deep water or routed out of seaweed (carefully) during a minus tide.

Observe size and sex restrictions on Dungeness crabs. Return undersized crabs to the water or to a spot where they can burrow for protection. Crabs left unprotected in the air can quickly dry out and die. In the San Juans it is illegal to collect or kill any live marine animal except for food use.

Chinaman Rock, on the northeast side of Shallow Bay is a striking example of the wave and chemical eroded sandstone and subsequent uplifting so characteristic of these northern isles. The rock is mostly obscured by a growth of trees, but can be found by going to the east end of the northernmost beach, then walking into the trees at the base of the cliff.

Body-sized hollows have been obviously geologically uplifted at least 30 feet since they were formed. The story goes that during the late 1800s Chinese aliens smuggled into the U.S. from Canada often hid in the recesses from patrolling immigration officials. Do not permit children to scratch names and deface the rock, so that others may enjoy this fascinating spot in its natural state.

Echo Bay, the largest on the island, contains fourteen mooring buoys, with ample space for additional boats to swing at anchor. Since this is the most open of Sucia anchorages, it can be uncomfortable during some wind and tide conditions. An additional stern hook can help secure the anchorage. The two long, forested islands in the bay, appropriately named North and South Finger Islands, are privately owned.

Boaters seeking privacy may find it in Ewing Cove, on the north side of Echo Bay. Although less protected and more difficult for larger boats to navigate, the cove nonetheless boasts the same rugged cliffs and sandy beaches which make the rest of the island so popular.

The outermost moorage buoy, when entering Ewing Cove, is over an underwater marine park area. Three sunken vessels are below the buoy and several yards to the east in 45 feet of water.

At Ewing Cove an added bonus for birdwatchers is Clements Reef and adjoining rocks, part of the San Juan Islands National Wilderness, and lying less than ½ mile to the north. Hundreds of sea birds congregate here, some of them nesting on Sucia and Matia, others merely resting in their migratory flights. Be content to identify them with strong binoculars from shore, for waters around the reef can be treacherous, and any approach by man disturbing to the birds. Seals, too, can be seen on the reefs, snoozing in the sun or warily eying passing boaters.

Looking inland, birdwatchers can often spot bald eagles perched high atop scraggly fir trees or soaring the skies above them. Although quite rare, brown pelicans have been seen here, foraging the shores. Double crested cormorants, known colloquially as "shags", sit on vacant buoys, overseeing harbor activities.

Cormorants are not completely waterproof, thus they must perch with wings hanging loosely or slightly outspread to dry their "sails". Their lack of oily waterproofing makes them less buoyant, enabling them to dive underwater to depths of several hundred feet to capture food. When winds are high, the cormorants can be seen with their long, black bodies plastered against sandstone cliffs; in good weather they frequently fly as flocks in sinuous V formations.

HIKING TRAILS

A dirt service road loops through the wooded main section of the island, with branch trails stretching from it to all ends of the island fingers. Except for park service equipment, motor vehicles or bicycles are prohibited on park roads and trails.

The trail around the north side of Fox Cove stays high on the bluff above the bay, while paths on Ev Henry Finger, Johnson Point and the north edge of Echo Bay skirt the water. Wear sturdy shoes on any long hike; deck "tennies" or sandals do not provide adequate footing on steep, slippery trails. Search shoreline rocks, especially on Ev Henry Finger, for fossilized clams, snails and ammonites 75 million years old. Such specimens may be collected, but digging in the banks with pick, shovel or any similar device is illegal.

The rock quarry near the service buildings at Fossil Bay is particularly dangerous and park personnel attempt to keep visitors out of the area. The loose cliffs are extremely hazardous to climb on; accidents have occurred here.

Cormorant

One of the most beautiful hikes on the island climbs to the top of Lawson Bluff on the northwest side of the island. Find the signed trail out of the northernmost campsite at Shallow Bay, near the latrines. A network of side trails makes the route confusing around the point; in general the best route lies along the edge of the bluff, overlooking the water. The trail climbs gradually upwards; in a few spots scrambly trails lead down to wave worn bedrock beaches. Keep a hand on the kids — the trail is easy enough, but in places it is so near the edge that a misstep could cause a bad fall.

The trail skirts the rim of the sheer bluff with aerial views of the ocean glimmering 100 feet below, the long stretch of Patos Island and the rugged outlines of the Canadian Gulf Islands. After about ¾ mile (1 km) the trail turns inland, joining the northernmost loop of the service road in another 200 yards. Turn right to return to Shallow Bay, left to reach the head of Echo Bay (the easiest return to Fossil Bay). Total distance of loop hike from Shallow Bay is about 1 mile (1½ km).

MATIA ISLAND

Island Area: 145 acres; Park Area 5 acres
Access: Boat only
Facilities: Dock with float, mooring buoys, water, picnic tables, pit toilets
Attractions: Clams, crabs, tide pools, fishing, beachcombing, hiking, scuba
diving

Although Matia may well be the loveliest of these jewel-like northern isles, it is often passed over by visiting boaters as it has limited overnight space. Only 5 acres facing on Rolfe Cove on the west end of the island are open to camping; the remainder is designated as National Wildlife Refuge.

The U.S. Fish and Wildlife Service permits use of the small area of the island as a state park, in the hopes that such limited use of the land will be compatible with wildlife preservation. If the presence of the public on Matia ever becomes a threat to the birds and mammals that live there and on nearby Puffin Island, all human intruders will be asked to pull up their tent stakes and anchors and go elsewhere. Treat the land with tender, loving care and strictly observe all regulations, or risk losing it.

Matia Island lies 2½ nautical miles northeast of Terrill Beach on Orcas Island, where boats may be rented or launched. For day excursions small boats can be beached in any of several coves of the island, however fires and overnight camping are allowed only on state park land.

Rolfe Cove holds a dock with a 45-foot float and a single mooring buoy, with room for only a few more boats to drop a hook. Hovering at the mouth of the cove, a rocky islet gives some protection from northerly winds. The bottom of

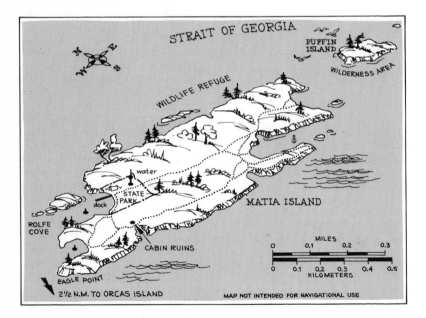

STRAIT OF GEORGIA

PUFFIN ISLAND

WILDERNESS AREA

WILDLIFE REFUGE

water

STATE PARK

dock

MATIA ISLAND

ROLFE COVE

CABIN RUINS

MILES
0   0.1   0.2   0.3

0   0.1   0.2   0.3   0.4   0.5
KILOMETERS

EAGLE POINT

2½ N.M. TO ORCAS ISLAND

MAP NOT INTENDED FOR NAVIGATIONAL USE

Rolfe Cove, Matia Island State Park

Rolfe Cove is deep and quite rocky; in a strong blow it may be difficult to secure a safe anchorage. The float is removed during the winter months to prevent damage from storms.

On the bank at the head of the cove are picnic tables, garbage cans, privys and space for about eight tents; water is supplied by a rustic hand pump located a few hundred feet down the trail.

The exposed walls of these coves are naturally sculptured masterpieces. Hollowed and smoothed by wind and waves, the stony banks are accentuated by banded patterns of layered conglomerate.

Boats may also anchor in a long, narrow bay on the east end of the island when tides are high; however, it is extremely shoal during summer low water. Several rocks lying in the entrance are an additional hazard.

"Matia" has undoubtedly the most varied and most disputed pronunciation of any San Juan Island. The Spanish pronunciation of the word, meaning "no protection", is Mah-*tee*-ah. However the name is often corrupted as May-shah, May-tee or Mat-ty.

In early years this island was the longtime home of one of the San Juan's most interesting characters, known as "the hermit of Matia". His name was Elvin Smith, and even though local newspapers of the day referred to him as a hermit,

Pigeon Guillemot

he was in truth not antisocial, for every week, in all but the foulest weather, he rowed his skiff to North Beach on Orcas Island. From here he hiked a 2-mile trail to East Sound to collect his mail, buy supplies and gossip with his cronies.

The pioneer recluse had gained a reputation as a mystic and mail-order faith healer. His weekly mail included dozens of letters, and sometimes money, from supplicants all over the country seeking his assistance. At home, on the retreat of his island, Smith claimed to spend hours each day in prayer on the behalf of his correspondents.

Elvin Smith lived for nearly 30 years on this briny paradise. From time to time other pioneers showed interest in the land, but one occupant on an 150-acre island was considered quite crowded enough at the time, so they settled elsewhere.

One stormy February in 1921, Smith, who was then 86, and a visiting friend, their boat heavily loaded with supplies, cast off from Orcas Island for the return trip to Matia. They were never seen again. Stones marking two vacant graves in an Orcas Island cemetery commemorate their lives.

Several trails on the island pass by the remnants of Smith's early settlement. A wide path leaves the dock at Rolfe Cove and heads south near the edge of the bay, reaching the cove near Eagle Cliff in about ½ mile. About 200 yards after leaving Rolfe Cove, a branch trail to the left leads to a diminutive bay. Debris of old buildings can be found near the marsh at the head of the cove.

The tree-shaded path continues eastward, edged by skeletons of ancient fences. Although Smith was a vegetarian, he kept sheep for wool, chickens for eggs, and rabbits, perhaps for companionship. Nearing the east end of the island, trails branch in many directions. One path reaches the head of a tiny vertical-walled inlet, others flank a long, mitten-shaped bay, climbing through wind-tormented madrona and hemlock to high bluffs.

This large, shallow cove may also be reached more directly by a ½-mile trail from Rolfe Cove by walking east on the trail past the water pump and through a brushy marsh. Clams may be dug in the tidal flat at the head of the bay.

One of the prettiest beaches in the island is a sandy crescent facing Puffin Island. To reach it, watch carefully for a branch trail on the left into the thick

Matia Island beach

brush at the tip of the "thumb" of the mitten-shaped bay. Within a few steps the bushes give way to the quiet of old-growth timber, where brackets of brilliant orange chicken-of-the-woods mushrooms can be found on decaying logs. Follow the trail east for ½ mile, staying in the flat, avoiding sketchy side trails going uphill on either side.

Sandy sections of the shore harbor clams. At low tide, rocks jutting out on the south side of the bay display spectacular tide pools, with multitudes of starfish, sea anemone, limpets, barnacles, tiny crabs and other creatures. Bring along a picnic lunch for all-day enjoyment of the island.

The bay looks out to Puffin Island, just a stone's throw offshore. The steep, rocky island, topped by a scraggly pompadour of trees and grass, is one of the islands of the San Juan Wilderness; going on shore is prohibited. Harbor seals and sea lions can often be seen lolling about in the warmth of the sun, and with binoculars squawking, gossipy sea birds can be identified — ungainly murres and auklets, bizarre puffins (known to some as sea parrots) and shy pigeon guillemots.

From mid-March to mid-September these birds gather in colonies and lay their single eggs in rock clefts, tending them until the downy chicks feather out and are able to fly. During this nesting time any close approach by boats or people is disturbing to the families; if the birds become alarmed by your presence, you are too close.

Early day Lummi Indians from the Bellingham region paddled dugout canoes to Matia and Puffin Islands to collect eggs, which they packed in the cool leaves of damp sea lettuce to safeguard against spoiling and breakage. The sea lettuce, too, was later eaten or dried for winter use. Today, visitors may sample the green, tissuey seaweed, but Uncle Sam protects the eggs.

I. THE NORTHERN BOUNDARY

CLARK ISLAND GROUP

Islands Area: 100 acres
Park Area: 56 acres
Access: Boat only
Facilities: Campsites, picnic tables, pit toilets, mooring buoys, *no water*
Attractions: Clams, mussels, beachcombing, skin diving, fishing, tide pools

Swept by the waters of the Straits of Georgia, overshadowed by the mountains of Orcas Island, a group of rocks and islands cluster together like the big brothers and small sisters of a family. On the southwest, the smaller, barren rocks are known as The Sisters, with the southernmost wedge-shaped rock named Little Sister. The largest of the rocks once sported a single pine tree, prompting the name Lone Tree Island, but the tree has long since surrendered to the sea, leaving the island to some tenacious grass and hundreds of nesting birds.

The Sisters are included in the San Juan Islands Wilderness. In spring and summer, cormorants, pigeon guillemots, gulls and other pelagic birds nest here. Other seasons gulls gather on the rocks, occasionally in great numbers, for reasons known only to gulls — perhaps an approaching storm, perhaps feeding is poor, perhaps for an afternoon coffee klatch. Whatever their reason, the cacophony of their conversation at such times is overwhelming, even on the shores of Clark Island.

Privately owned Barnes Island lies on the west of the island group, while less than ½ mile to the east is the largest of the family, Clark Island, a marine state park. Although located less than 2 miles from the shores of Orcas Island, the nearest public boat launching area is 5 nautical miles to the west at North Beach. The distance from populated areas, the lack of fresh water for campers and the lack of protected anchorages makes this one of the less-frequented of the San Juan marine state parks.

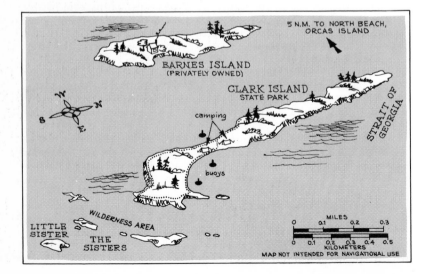

Clark Island beach

217

Clark Island State Park; Barnes Island on right

The slender island is a mile in length, but scarcely 300 yards across at its widest point. Its southern end hooks sharply eastward to form a broad bay; here six mooring buoys offer easy anchorages. Boaters approaching this bay should use care, as several rocks lie just beneath the water surface where boats have been known to run aground. Refer to a good navigational chart for location of hazards. A slight indentation on the opposite side of the island holds three additional mooring buoys, somewhat sheltered by Barnes Island.

Campers may pitch tents in one of six campsites above the beach on the east side of the island. Two more campsites can be found in the trees along the cross-island trail which connects the two anchorages. The west beach is a day use picnic area. Camping or building fires on the beach is prohibited in order to keep it as natural as possible.

Timber on the southern end of the island is sparse, with graceful red-barked madronas leaning over the banks. A bluff-top trail can be followed around this end of the island, with views down to beaches and tiny steep-walled coves; numerous side trails drop down to the water.

Clark Island is reputed to have the nicest beaches of any of these northern island state parks. Sandy flats to the south, exposed at low tide, are good for clamming and summertime wading. Mussels cling to protruding rocks. The steeper, rocky northern beaches hold an array of marine life — purple starfish, pastel sea anemone, barnacles, sea squirts, purple and green sea urchins and more — to be admired by skin divers and tide pool explorers.

EMERGENCY PHONE NUMBERS AND LIST OF CONTACTS

FIRE (ALARMS ONLY)

Fidalgo Island—293-3155
Lopez Island—468-2555
Orcas Island—376-2341
San Juan Island—378-4341
Shaw Island—468-2500
For fires on remote islands, call the Department of Natural Resources—1-(800)-562-6010 (If calling by radio, notify Coast Guard)

MEDICAL EMERGENCIES

Fidalgo Island—293-3181
Lopez Island—468-2333
Orcas Island—376-2341
San Juan Island—378-2117

SHERIFF

Fidalgo Island—336-3146
Lopez Island—468-2333
Orcas Island—376-2207
San Juan Island—378-4141

U.S. COAST GUARD

Anacortes—293-9555

RADIO CONTACTS

Marine V.H.F.: Coast Guard distress or hailing—Channel 16
Coast Guard liason—Channel 22A

Citizens Band: Distress—Channel 9

U.S. CUSTOMS

Friday Harbor—378-2080 (after hours—378-4677)
Anacortes—293-2331

WASHINGTON STATE FERRIES

Information (Seattle)—464-6400
Anacortes terminal—293-2188
Lopez terminal—468-2252
Orcas terminal—376-4389
Friday Harbor terminal—378-4777
Shaw terminal—468-2288

PARKS

San Juan National Historical Park: S.J. Zachwieja, Supt.; P.O. Box 549; Friday Harbor, Wa. 98250. Phone—378-2240

Washington State Parks and Recreation Information Service: P.O. Box 1128: Olympia, Wa. 98501. Phone—1-(800)-562-8200 (toll free).

Northern San Juan State Parks (Sucia I., Matia I., Clark I., Patos I., Freeman I.): Bill Byrne, Ranger; Eastsound, Wa. 98245. Phone—376-4698.

Eastern San Juan State Parks (Spencer Spit, James I., Saddlebag I., Turn I., Doe I.): Doug Pesznecker, Ranger; Lopez Island, Wa. 98261. Phone—468-2251.

Western San Juan State Parks (Reid Harbor, Prevost Harbor, Turn Point, Jones I., Posey I., Lime Kiln Lighthouse): Wil Lorentz, Manager; 6158 Lighthouse Road, Friday Harbor, Wa. 98250. Phone—378-2044.

Deception Pass State Park: Ralph Mast, Ranger: 5175 N. State Highway 20: Oak Harbor, Wa. 98275. Phone—675-2417.

Moran State Park: Dave Hoffman, Manager: Eastsound, Wa.; 98245. Phone—376-2326.

San Juan County Park: Al Surina, Manager; Friday Harbor, Wa. 98250. Phone—378-2992.

Odlin County Park: Kevin Murphy, Caretaker; Lopez Island, Wa. 98261. Phone—468-2496.

NAUTICAL CHARTS AND MAPS

Sketch maps in this book are intended for general orientation only. When traveling by boat on any of the San Juan waters it is imperative that the appropriate nautical charts be used. The following list of charts covers the areas included in this book. They may be purchased at map stores or many marine supply centers.

NOAA Chart 18423, Bellingham to Everett, including San Juan Islands (Scale 1:80,000 — folio of charts, including some detailed insets.)

NOAA Chart 18421, Strait of Juan de Fuca to Strait of Georgia (Scale 1:80,000 — covers all areas included in this book.)

NOAA Chart 18424, Bellingham Bay (Scale 1:40,000)

NOAA Chart 18427, Anacortes to Skagit Bay (Scale 1:25,000)

NOAA Chart 18425, Friday and Roche Harbors (Scale 1:20,000)

Although it would be difficult to get seriously lost on any of the islands, the USGS topographical maps listed below are useful and interesting. Maps noted with a (P) are black and white 7½' preprints, which will eventually become available as full color maps, but at this time must be ordered from the U.S. Geological Survey, 345 Middlefield Road, Menlo Park, Ca. All other topographical maps are available at hiking or map stores.

15' series maps — Deception Pass, Orcas Island.

7½' series maps — Anacortes North, Anacortes South (P), Crescent Harbor, Lummi Island, Cypress Island, Deception Pass, Mt. Constitution (P), Blakely Island, Lopez Pass, Eastsound, Shaw Island, Richardson, Waldron Island, Friday Harbor, False Bay, Stuart Island, Roche Harbor.

INDEX

OTHER BOOKS IN THE "HIKES" SERIES:

50 Hikes in Mount Rainier National Park
101 Hikes in the North Cascades
102 Hikes in the Alpine Lakes, South Cascades and Olympics
Companion volumes guide you to the best hiking in the mountains of Washington State
. . . valleys and ridges, forests, glacier views, subalpine meadows, ice caves and
snowfields. Easy-to-use sketch maps and complete trail directions. "101" covers from
Stevens Pass to the Canadian Border. "102" covers from Stevens Pass south to the
Columbia River. "50" includes the Wonderland Trail and Mount Rainier. Text by Harvey
Manning, photos by Bob and Ira Spring.

103 Hikes in Southwestern British Columbia
The most scenic trips from Vancouver Island to Manning Park, from the U.S. Border to
Lytton at the head of the Fraser Canyon. (Includes Garibaldi Park.) Maps and photos for
each trip. Prepared by the B.C. Mountaineering Club, with text by David Macaree, maps
by Mary Macaree.

109 Walks in B.C.'s Lower Mainland
Delightful walks to see the best in Vancouver and vicinity. Complete directions and
maps for each trip; scenic photos of the highlights. Text by David Macaree, photos by
Mary Macaree.

**Trips and Trails, 1: Family Camps, Short Hikes and View Roads Around the North
Cascades**
**Trips and Trails, 2: Family Camps, Short Hikes and View Roads in the Olympics,
Mt. Rainier and South Cascades**
Companion volumes geared for beginner hikers and families, with maps, photos and
complete trail directions for short hikes (under two miles) starting from campgrounds.
Also describes facilities of each campground. "1" includes the San Juan, Whidbey and
Fidalgo Island areas. By E.M. Sterling, photos by Bob and Ira Spring, maps by Marge
Mueller.

Bicycling the Backroads Around Puget Sound
Bicycling the Backroads of Northwest Washington
Full details, maps on cycle tours on quiet backroads, including scenery, mileages,
elevation change, estimated times. Companion volumes, no duplication of trips. By Erin
and Bill Woods.

Footsore 1, 2, 3 and 4: Walks and Hikes Around Puget Sound
A four-volume series concentrating on pockets and stretches of wild lands near civiliza-
tion, taking the explorer along beaches, backroads, and trails among mountain foothills.
Trips range from short and easy to all-day hikes requiring boots, a map, and experience.
By Harvey Manning, with photos by Bob and Ira Spring. **F,1** covers Seattle, the
Sammamish Valley, Issaquah Alps. **F,2** covers the Snoqualmie, Tolt and Skykomish
River valleys. **F,3** covers the Stillaguamish and Skagit River valleys, Camano, Whidbey
and Fidalgo Islands, North Kitsap and Olympic Peninsulas. **F,4** covers the valleys of the
Carbon, Puyallup, Nisqually and Deschutes Rivers, South Kitsap and Olympic Penin-
sulas.